SPLENDORS OF
ROME
AND VATICAN

TULLIO POLIDORI

CONTENTS

page   *3 - Foreword*
»   *4 - The growth of Rome*

FIRST TOUR   **Borghese Gallery, the Pantheon, Basilica of Saint Peter.**
»   *6 - Borghese Gallery*
»   *15 - The Pincio*
»   *17 - From Pincio garden to the Spanish Steps*
»   *18 - Piazza di Spagna*
»   *19 - Campo Marzio and Piazza Navona*
»   *26 - The Pantheon*
»   *29 - From Pantheon to St. Peter's Basilica*
»   *34 - Basilica of Saint Peter in the Vatican*

SECOND TOUR   **Vatican Museums and the Sistine Chapel**
page   *42 - The statues and the Court of Belvedere*
»   *44 - Raphael Stanzas*
»   *50 - Sistine Chapel*

THIRD TOUR   **Piazza della Repubblica, Trevi Fountain, the Forum, the Colosseum, Saint Paul's without the Walls**
page   *65 - Piazza della Repubblica and the Thermae Museum*
»   *67 - Largo di Santa Susanna*
»   *68 - The Quirinal*
»   *71 - Trevi Fountain*
»   *73 - Piazza Venezia*
»   *75 - Marcellus Theatre*
»   *77 - Piazza Bocca della Verità and the Tiber Island*
»   *79 - The Capitol*
»   *84   The Roman Forum*
»   *100 - Avenue of the Imperial Fora*
»   *104 - Colosseum*
»   *111 - The Circus Maximus*
»   *114 - Basilica of Saint Paul's without the Walls*

FOURTH TOUR   **Basilica of Santa Maria Maggiore, Saint Peter in Chains and Michelangelo's Moses, the Holy Stairs and Saint John Lateran, Appian Way and the Catacombs, Janiculum and Trastevere.**
page   *118 - Basilica of Sainta Maria Maggiore (St. Mary Major)*
»   *123 - San Pietro in Vincoli (St. Peter in Chains) and Michelangelo's Moses*
»   *125 - Scala Santa (the Holy Stairs) and St. John Lateran*
»   *129 - Caracalla's Baths and the Ancient Appian Way*
»   *130 - Catacombs of St. Calixtus*
»   *131 - Catacombs of St. Sebastion*
»   *132 - Catacombs of St. Domitilla*
»   *134 - Janiculum and Trastevere*

FIFTH TOUR   **Tivoli, Hadrian's Villa and Villa d'Este**
page   *136 - Hadrian's Villa*
»   *139 - Villa d'Este*

FOREWORD

This guide to Rome seeks to offer the visitor a clear picture, and one that is as exhaustive as possible within the limits of space, of the places which are worthy of note, according to a pattern of visits which is in keeping with the traditional routes organised by the major tourist agencies.

The short stretch of time which the tourist usually has available to him is not enough to visit the countless churches and monuments which are usually listed in the majority of publications of this kind, and a detailed description, accompanied by a dry list of names and dates, in no way conveys the fascination of Rome, which is a unique city. So in this guide an essential selection has been made, leaving out details and facts which might only serve to produce confusion, and thus giving the memory more freedom to fix on sharply-defined images of works and monuments which are really important and typical. For this reason we have aimed at a straightforward and simple style, avoiding any kind of rhetoric, to show the spirit of a civilisation which the visitor will want to retain in his mind's eye so as to return to it over and over again in the imagination.

We have also sought to show the connections and relations betwen monuments, historical facts, and famous people who have been responsible for their construction. In this context the historical reasons, as well as the political and religious ones, play their role as an expression of humanity, linking the past to the present and, we hope, inspiring the visitor with a spark of love for Rome and for its history.

L' INSEGNE DELLI XIIII   *Scala modulatoria de paſsi 1000. che fanno uno miglio Italiano*   RIONI O REGIONI DI ROMA.
Piede Romano, de quali 5. fanno il Paſso.   *se vend A AMSTERDAM chez PIERRE MORTIER.*

S.ANGELO   PIGNA   CAMPIDELLI   TRASTEVERE   REGOLA   S.EUSTACHIO   MONTI   COLONNA   PONTE   RIPA   TRIVIO   PARIONE   CAMPOMARZO   BORGO

C   D   E   F   G

Museum of the Palazzo dei Conservatori. The Capitoline Wolf: Etruscan sculpture of the 6th century. The twins were added in the 15th century by Pollaiuolo.

THE GROWTH OF ROME

According to Varro, Rome was founded on April 21st 753 BC, when Romulus and his shepherds settled on the Palatine Hill; eventually they expanded on to the Capitol, the Quirinal, the Viminal, the Esquiline, Caelian and Aventine Hills on the south — Rome's seven hills, all standing on the left bank of the Tiber.

753-510 BC **The firts period under the Kings.** Rome expanded into the Latium area, through wars with the Sabines, Fideneans, Veientes, Latins and Etruscans.

510-29 BC **Under the Republic.** Rome continued to develop and expand throughout the peninsula, with battles against other races already settled there. In the Mediterranean there was an epic struggle with Carthage which began in 264 BC, and ended in 146 when Carthage was razed to the ground. In addition to this the Romans conquered Spain, Illyria, Macedonia, Greece and Asia Minor, and lastly Gaul, at the hands of Julius Cae

sar, who in fact put an end to the Republic. He was assassinated by stabbing in 44 BC.

29 BC - 475 AD: The period of the Roman Empire. This was marked by a first phase of splendour, lasting for about two hundred years, during which the authority of Rome was extended to Mauretania, Britain, Fresia and Dacia. However, from the third century a gradual period of decay began, and this culminated whit the fall of the Roman Empire in the West.

Principal Events of this third period:
(A.D.)

14   Death of Augustus. The great peace-loving Emperor devoted much care and attention to Rome, so that he could justly boast of having found a city of bricks and left one of marble.

64   The burning of Rome under Nero.

70   The conquest of Jerusalem by Titus.

117   Death of Trajan, under whom the Empire reached its greatest extent, and the city of Rome had about one and a half million inhabitants.

272   Aurelian, worried by the threatened invasion of Italy by the barbarians, began the construction of the defensive walls around Rome.

312   Victory of Constantine over Maxentius.

313   Promulgation of the Edict of Milan, by which Constantine granted the Christians freedom of worship, thus ending the age of persecutions.

331   Transfer of the capital of the Empire to Byzantium (Constantinople) to make the defence of the eastern boundaries of the Empire stronger.

410   First sack of Rome by the Visigoths under Alaric.

455   Second sack of Rome by the Vandals under Genseric.

471   Third sack of Rome by Ricimer at the head of the armies of the Arian Germans.

View of Rome from Monte Mario.

476	Deposition of the last Roman Emperor Romulus Augustulus, at the hands of Odoacer, a Danubian soldier of fortune, who was acclaimed head of the barbarian armies by various tribes — the Eruli, Rugi and Scyrians.
476	to approximately 1400: **The Mediaeval Period.** The history of Rome is linked to the groving self-assertion of the Popes as spiritual head of the whole Church and as de facto sovereign of the city.

Main Events:

493-553	Domination of the Goths in Italy, during which the prestige of the Bishop of Rome grew constantly.
536-553	War between the Goths and Byzantium. Rome, occupied first by one army and then by the other, eventually fell permanently into the hands of the Byzantines. During thcir dominance the Popes created the basis for their claims to temporal power.
568-774	Dominance of Italy by the Lombards.
728	Donation by the Lombard king Liutprand of the Castle of Sutri to the Blessed Apostles Peter and Paul. This was the actual beginning of the temporal power of the Popes.
756	Pepin, King of the Franks, assigned to the Pope the lands taken by the Lombards from the Byzantines. Subsequently the Papal State was created, including the Duchy of Rome and other territories.
774	Defeat of the Lombards by Charlemagne.
800	Coronation of Charlemagne in Saint Peter's as Emperor of the Holy Roman Empire, which included almost the whole of Western Europe in its area.
1300	Proclamation of the first Jubilee Year by Boniface VIII.
1308-1377	Period of the «Babylonian Captivity» of the Popes in Avignon. As a result of this Rome fell into decay and lost much of its importance; its population sunk as low as 20,000 people.

The Renaissance. Occupies roughly the fifteenth, sixteenth and part of the seventeenth centuries. It is characterised by an intensive activity on the part of the Popes who sought to adorn the city of Rome; they summoned famous artists like Bramante (1444-1514); Michelangelo (1475-1564); Raphael (1483-1520) to Rome, and in their works these artists expressed the zeal for perfection and grace which is the hallmark of the Renaissance.

1447	The list of Renaissance Popes begins with Nicholas V.
1506	Pope Julius II laid the first stone of the new Basilica of S. Peter's.
1626	Pope Urban VIII consecrated the new church of S. Peters', the greatest witness to the committement given by the Popes of the sixteenth century and the taste of the Renaissance — all aimed at the attainment of an ideal of refined beauty and classical décorum. During the whole of the 17th century Rome was constantly embellished by works of the baroque style — especially at the hands of Bernini (1598-1680).

The Risorgimento Period and the Modern Age.

1870	End of the Temporal Power and proclamation of Rome as the Capital of Italy.
1929-1943	Rome, where the Fascist government was established, felt the impact of the Roman Imperialistic pretensions of the régime. Grandiose projects such as EUR grew up, and little by little the picturesque aspect of the city gave way to the retorical style of the lictors, aimed at giving prominence to massive and showy architectural structures making generous use of marble.

During the Second World War Rome was declared an Open City; thanks to this privilege, hundreds of thousands of refugees escaped there from all parts of Italy, and many of them stayed when the war ended. Today Rome's population is over three million.

Borghese Gallery - The Pantheon - St. Peter's

There are not many places in the world where the survival of the past is as tangible as in Rome, with all its ruins disseminated a little everywhere, reminding one of ancient glorious times, and with its countless architectural palimpsests. Of all the antiquities, the one you see most frequently during your stay in the Eternal City, and of which so little is said, is the **Aurelian Wall,** the defence wall built by Emperor Aurelianus in 272 A.D. The ancestor of all the town walls in Europe was built to protect the capital of the Roman Empire when the threat of the barbarian invasions appeared more determined. It was nineteen kilometers in perimeter, had three hundred towers, two thousand small windows and was pierced by fourteen main gates in correspondence to the roads starting from Rome. A conspicuous sector of the mighty wall stands at the top of **Via Veneto,** too solemn a background for the fancy sidewalk cafés and the international high-life on this street.

Beyond this part of the indented wall and its old gate, **Porta Pinciana,** we enter the beautiful **Villa Borghese,** the biggest city-park, miraculously saved from the increasing demands of housing construction. This park was, for a few hundred years, the private property of the Borghese family, still one of the leading families of the Italian nobility.

A view of the Aurelian Walls.

Via Veneto.

Borghese Gallery

About five minutes walk from Porta Pinciana, still partly hidden by the umbrella pines and the ilex groves, we discover the **Casino Borghese,** the summer house built for Cardinal Scipione Borghese which was used mainly for receptions and parties. The Borghese family still lives in the palace built by the Cardinal in the center of Rome, and the villa was built in 1613, soon after the lay-out of the park had been designed by the Dutch architect Johan Van Santen, who italicised his name into Giovanni Vasanzio.

The Villa was transformed into a museum in 1902, when it was sold to the State, along with the private art collection and the Park. Cardinal Scipione Borghese was the nephew of another prominent member of this family, Pope Paul V.

When entering the museum we are overwhelmed by the fresco painting on the ceiling of the entrance hall; it is the work of a Sicilian-born artist, Mariano Rossi, XVIII century, depicting events from Roman history and pagan mythology. On the floor we notice five mosaics, dating from the third century A.D. and found at Torrenova, near Tusculum, a few miles from Rome.

They represent the fights of the gladiators and the hunting of wild animals — combats of the arena. Near the walls are numerous statues from Roman times, of pagan divinities and emperors. Throughout the gallery is a large display of valuable marbles and antiquities all recovered from the ruins. These innumerable works of art the patrician families of Rome rescued and they used them to decorate their sumptuous homes. But the important reason for us to come to, this museum is to see the portrait of Pauline Bonaparte by Canova, a few statues by Bernini and some paintings of importance on the first floor. We go first to the right, to the room where, reclining as a Venus on an Empire couch and holding the apple of Paris in one hand, is **Pauline Bonaparte,** the youngest sister of Napoleon who was married to Prince Camillo Borghese. This world-famous masterpiece is the por-

Portrait of Cardinal Scipione Borghese by Bernini, in the Borghese Gallery.

The Casino Borghese, Principal Façade.

Pauline Bonaparte by Canova.

trait she commissioned from Antonio Canova, the leader of the Neo-Classical style of the 19th century. It is one of the finest examples of this style which bloomed actually as a reaction to the exaggerations of the Baroque style, by which it was preceded. The Neo-Classical style was a new revival of Grecian and Roman art, an imitation of classic art, which always remained a little cold; the statue of Pauline is the only exception. In the lovely figure, all grace and charm, in the softness of the various details, you hardly notice that the sculptor strictly follows the canons of classic art. This is the best work by Canova, it certainly also depended on the personality of the model. The fact that Pauline posed naked was taken as an outrage by the Borghese family, but she would not pay much attention to their criticism, modesty, as we know, not being her main virtue.

In the next room is the statue of **David** by **Gian Lorenzo Bernini.** Bernini (1598 - 1680), at the age of seven moved to Rome, where he spent the rest of his life. He was primarily a sculptor, like his father Pietro Bernini, a talented artist of the late Renaissance, but young Lorenzo had the versatility of the great Renaissance masters, and turned his genius to architecture and painting as well. In his long life he served eight Popes and made of Rome a Baroque city. This statue he executed on commission by his admirer and patron, Cardinal Scipione in 1623-24, when he was only 25-years old. For this David he chose the moment of action before the hurling of the stone against Goliath. The figure is freely moving in space, and is extremely realistic; Bernini has transfused in the marble the impetuosity, the fury and the determination of the biblical hero. The face is a self-portrait. David's extreme realism and movement were the innovations which announced the birth of the style known as **Baroque** (from Spanish «barrueco», which means irregular in form, especially said of pearls), of which Bernini is the acknowledged father. Bernini broke away from the traditional manneristic style.

Apollo and Daphne by Gian Lorenzo Bernini.

Gian Lorenzo Bernini – The Rape of Proserpina.

We pass to the next room where we find the group of **Apollo and Daphne,** which Bernini made also for Cardinal Scipione Borghese in the following year.

The pagan legend of Apollo chasing the lovely nymph, made into a laurel tree when she was overtaken, is represented in the moment of the metamorphosis. Bernini's talent appears more evident in this work; we note his extraordinary technical skill in giving all the minute details and the exact texture of the various parts from one single piece of marble. We read the expression of horror and amazement on their faces. Although there are some classical reminiscences, the work has all of Bernini's temperament. (Compare this one with the Apollo Belvedere at the Vatican).

Through a small room, which had been a private chapel, we pass into the Sala degli Imperatori (the room of the Emperors). This resplendent room, decorated all around with porphyry and alabaster busts of Roman Emperors copied from Roman portraits, is dominated by the group of **Pluto and Proserpina,** in the center, also by Bernini. This sculpture, which preceded the other two, shows in its technical virtuosity (the hand of Pluto sinking into the soft flesh of Persephone, the tears, etc.) the influence of mannerism, but the softness of Persephone's figure, the movement, the vigour and the violence show Bernini's exuberance and anticipate his innovations and his freedom of creation.

The Baroque style prevailed for about two hundred years; due to the exaggerations of Bernini's followers, the style fell into ostentation and became too showy and theatrical; the spontaneous reaction to it was, as we saw, the Neo-Classical style of the 19th century.

The actual picture gallery is on the upper floor. In the room opposite the top of the staircase we find three Paintings by Raphaels.

A **Deposition,** signed and dated 1507, commissioned to him by Atalanta Baglioni to commemorate her dead son. A beautifully proportioned composition, but its extreme balance has weakened the profound

The Borghese Gallery – the Sala degli Imperatori, or Room of the Emperors.

Portrait of Young Woman, Raphael.

David, by Bernini.

which seem to support the roof. This is called the Room of Caravaggio, whose paintings are recognisable by the sharp contrast of light and the realism of his Saints and Madonnas; because of this realism the Church refused some of his sacred representations, but Caravaggio's new manner was to prevail, and Cardinal Scipione Borghese himself bought the picture of the **Madonna dei Palafrenieri** which hangs on one of the end walls. Next to it, by the window, is the **David with Goliath's Head,** the head of Goliath being a dramatic self-portrait. Two more works by Caravaggio in this room are **The Boy with Basket of Fruit** and the **Young Bacchus ill,** another self-portrait when the artist had malaria. Caravaggio lived a short but adventurous life; he died at the age of 37 in 1610. He opened new ways for European painting. On the opposite end wall is the large painting of **the Hunting of Diana** by Domenichino, XVII century, a typical manneristic work.

This room also contains some works by Bernini. The portrait, an excellent one, of **Cardinal Scipione Bor-**

sense of grief, the main theme of the picture.

A **Portrait of Young Woman with the Unicorn**, this picture had been painted over to represent St. Catherine; restorations proved Raphael's authorship.

A **Portrait of Man**, which also had been painted over and again restorations revealed Raphael's hand. On the opposite wall is the **Madonna and Child** by Botticelli, not one of his greatest works, but it has Botticelli's charm and the accuracy of design typical of Florentine art. Another **Madonna and Child** by Perugino, the teacher of Raphael, and next to it a **Crucifixion** by Pinturicchio, the other leading painter of the Umbrian School — XV century. In this picture is a lovely Umbrian landscape, with St. Christopher fording the river carrying the Child on his shoulder, in the foreground.

We return to the stairs and enter the large central room, which was decorated on the ceiling by Giovanni Lanfranco in the XVII century, depicting the gods of the Olympus, and all around the caryatids,

The Deposition by Raphael.

ghese, perfect in the physical features and in the psychology of the subject; a replica of this portrait is at the other end of the same wall; Bernini made it in fifteen days, for the original cracked because of a flaw in the marble. There is also the terracotta model for the equestrian monument to Louis XIV which was never executed.

Through a small room containing three paintings by Bernini and one by Rubens, we reach the room of the **Danae** by Correggio, another gem of this collec-tion. This prominent painter of the XVI century, from Parma, is, by some authorities, considered to be almost as great as Titian for the handling of colors. The painting has a most wonderful golden, hazy luminescence, irradiating from the golden cloud into which Jupiter had transformed himself to enter Danae's prison.

A good study of color in the mysterious **Circe,** by Dosso Dossi from Ferrara, XVI century (on the op-posite wall).

Boy with basket of fruit, Caravaggio.

Sacred and Profane Love, Titian.

The culmination of the whole gallery is in the next room.

It is the most famous **Sacred and Profane Love** by Titian, which everyone knows from reproductions, but no reproduction can prepare you for the perfect rendering of the brilliant silk draperies, the radiant fleshy tints and the warm, clear light. The Sacred and Profane Love is an early work by Titian, who died at the age of 99; the other three works in this room are of the last period.

The **Scourging of Christ** is a late picture in which the suffering and pain are expressed through color and light effects. The study of color also prevails in the spiritual struggle of **St. Dominic** and in the painting of **Venus Blindfolding Love.**

Now we retrace our steps to the stairs and then to the exit. Our drive will take us across the Gardens of Villa Borghese, which appears more of an English landscaped park than a formal Italian garden; the layout of the park was redesigned by the Scottish artist Jacob More and the Italian Camporese in the XVIII century.

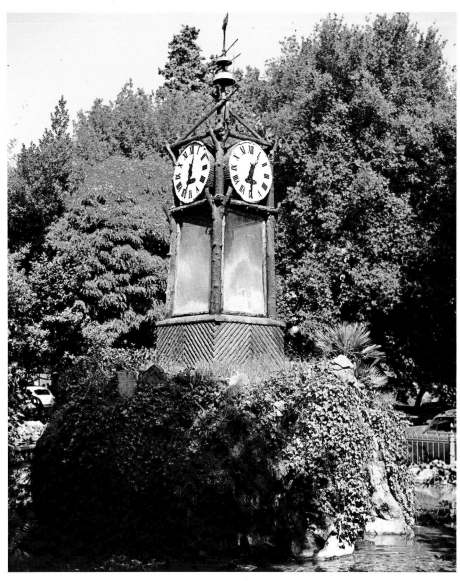

The Pincio; The Water Clock.

The Pincio

After a brief look at the water clock, (a curiosity of this park), we stop on the great terrace known as the Piazzale Napoleone I. **The Pincio Garden**, as it now appears, was laid out by order of Napoleon Bonaparte, around the villa he built for his son, the King of Rome. In Roman times this area was owned by the Pinci family, and here were the gardens of Lucullus. From this terrace we enjoy one of the famous views of Rome, dominated by St. Peter's dome. Below the terrace lies the beautiful **Piazza del Popolo**, its center marked by the Egyptian obelisk which Augustus brought to Rome two thousand years ago, when it already was an antique, for it dates from the thir-

teenth century B.C. Down on the left are the twin Churches by Rainaldi, Santa Maria in Montesanto and Santa Maria dei Miracoli, while on the right is the much more interesting church of **Santa Maria del Popolo**, one of the museum churches of Rome. There are works by most eminent artists, such as Bramante, Bregno, Pinturicchio, Raphael, Sansovino, Caravaggio, etc. This is the church where Martin Luther celebrated his first Roman Mass. In the distance you discover several highlights of Rome; if you have extra time it would be worth coming to Monte Pincio to watch the sun setting behind St. Peter's.

On leaving the Pincio we'll pass by the **Villa Medici**, built by Annibale Lippi in 1554 for Cardinal Ricci and then bought by a Cardinal Ferdinando de' Medici in 1580; it was sold to Napoleon in 1803 and it houses the French Academy. In the Villa Medici Galileo was held by the Inquisition.

As we pass the church of **Trinità dei Monti,** founded by King Charles VIII of France, we can look down over the **Spanish Steps** and, continuing through via Sistina, the street built by Sixtus V, which leads to Santa Maria Maggiore, we drive as far as **Piazza Barberini**, where there are two charming fountains by Bernini: the **Fountain of the Triton**, a sea monster blowing a conch and seated on an open sea shell, and the **Fountain of the Bees**, Fontana delle Api.

From Monte Pincio to the Spanish Steps

Piazza Barberini by night.

View of the Piazza del Popolo from the Pincio terrace. In the background, the dome of St. Peter's.

«The Triton» by Bernini. Detail of the Triton Fountain, in Piazza Barberini.

The Villa Medici.

The Spanish Steps

Piazza di Spagna. Springtime display of azaleas and paintings.

The Keats-Shelley Museum.

A superb panorama of Rome from the top of Trinità dei Monti.

▲ A «violin solo» on the Spanish Steps.

▲ Piazza di Spagna: The «Old Boat» Fountain of Pietro Bernini.

The spring sunshine invites you to linger awhile on the steps of Trinità dei Monti. ▼

◄ Trinità dei Monti and detail of the Boat Fountain.

Hippies. ▼

The «Caffé Greco» in Via Condotti.

Through Via del Tritone and Via Due Macelli, we reach **Piazza di Spagna**, which for three centuries has been the tourist center of Rome. In its neighbourhood lodged Byron, Liszt, Goethe. Angelika Kauffman, Stendhal, Balzac, Hans Andersen and many others. The English poet Keats died in the house at the foot of the Spanish Steps on the right hand side. These steps should actually be named the French Steps, for the artistic staircase built in 1723, was the donation of a French diplomat, Etienne Gouffier. It was designed by the architects De Sanctis and Specchi, the latter beeing also responsible for the palace of the Spanish Embassy to the Holy See, from which the Piazza takes its name.

In front of the Spanish Embassy stands the Roman column supporting the statue of the Immaculate Conception, this monument commemorates the promulgation of the Dogma of the Immaculate Conception, by Pope Pius IX in 1854. Piazza di Spagna is also the heart of the smartest shopping center and the artists' quarter; many of them live on Via Margutta and Via del Babuino, which leads to Piazza del Popolo. In these two streets you also find many antique shops and fine arts dealers. **The fountain of the Barcaccia**, the Old Barge, is the work of Bernini's father, XVI century. We enter Via dei Condotti, which is famous for its jewellers and most exclusive shops; almost immediately on the right is the Caffè Greco, which was

The interior of «Caffé Greco» in a painting by Ludwig Passini, 1852.
(Kunst Halle, Hamburg).

21

Museum of the Baths of Diocletian: Statue of Caesar August from the via Labicana. Detail.

The ruins of the mausoleum of Augustus.

Piazza Augusto Imperatore

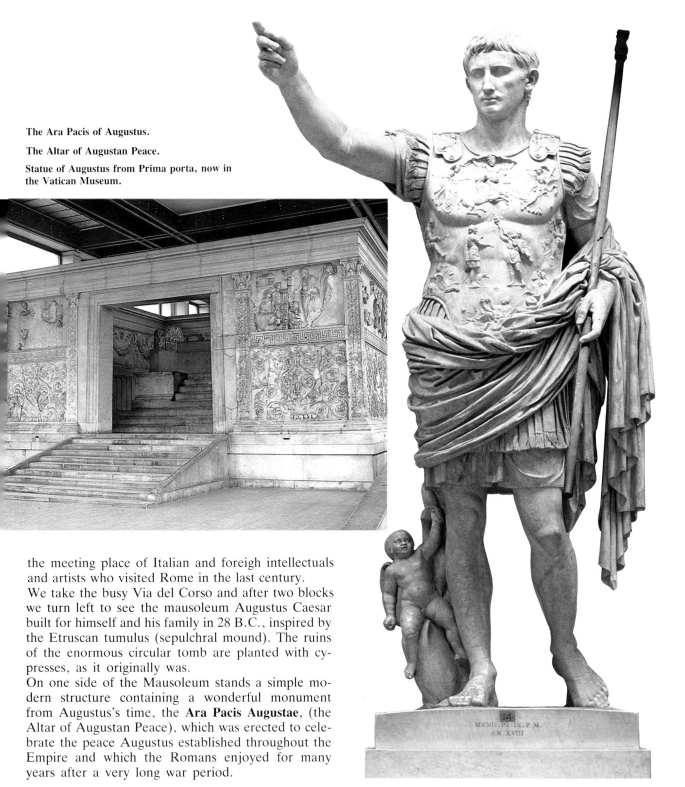

The Ara Pacis of Augustus.

The Altar of Augustan Peace.

Statue of Augustus from Prima porta, now in the Vatican Museum.

the meeting place of Italian and foreigh intellectuals and artists who visited Rome in the last century.

We take the busy Via del Corso and after two blocks we turn left to see the mausoleum Augustus Caesar built for himself and his family in 28 B.C., inspired by the Etruscan tumulus (sepulchral mound). The ruins of the enormous circular tomb are planted with cypresses, as it originally was.

On one side of the Mausoleum stands a simple modern structure containing a wonderful monument from Augustus's time, the **Ara Pacis Augustae**, (the Altar of Augustan Peace), which was erected to celebrate the peace Augustus established throughout the Empire and which the Romans enjoyed for many years after a very long war period.

Campo Marzio and Piazza Navona

We now enter the old historical section still called **Campo Marzio** (The Field of Mars — the god of war). This is the area where the legions were encamped during the Roman Republic; under the Caesars it was occupied by different public buildings, such as temples, stadiums, theaters etc. (Julius Caesar was stabbed to death in the Theater of Pompey which was where the church of St. Andrew now stands. In this area is **Piazza Navona**, which is one of the most superb squares of Rome, built over the ruins of the Stadium of Domitian of which has kept the elliptical shape of the racing track.

It is decorated with three baroque fountains, the central one, the **Fountain of the Four Rivers**, is another product of Bernini's exuberant genius. The four allegorical figures represent the Nile, the Ganges, the

Piazza Navona in its splendid
Baroque setting.

Night view of the Bernini
Fountain of Four Rivers.

Danube and the River Plate. The monumental facade
of **the church of S. Agnese in Agone** is the work of
Bernini's rival, Borromini; a popular legend relates
that Bernini's River Plate raises his hand so as to
prevent the church from falling, but this was unveiled
in 1651 and the church was only completed in 1666,
so the legend does not correspond to fact.
We pass the **Palazzo Madama**, a beautiful XVII century building, now the seat of the Senate, and the
Palazzo della Sapienza, which was the Roman University until 1935, built by Giacomo della Porta and Borromini (the rival of Bernini) and finally we reach the
Pantheon.

The Pantheon

M. 43,30

The most important monument in the Campus Martius is the **Pantheon**, which is the only architectural relic from imperial Rome that has remained intact to us with doors and roof, surviving the wreckage of eighteen centuries. Pantheon is a Greek word meaning «all the gods» and the temple was dedicated to the main planetarian divinities and was built first by Agrippa between 27 and 25 B.C. The present temple is the one Emperor Hadrian rebuilt between 120 and 125 A.D. and probably designed by the Emperor himself. Its perfect state of preservation is due to the fact that it was consecrated as a church dedicated to St. Mary of All Martyrs in 608 by Pope Boniface IV who received it from the Byzantine Emperor Phocas. The powerful structure is also one of the most harmonius buildings, unusual in its exterior with the pediment porch reminding one of a Greek temple and adjoining a classic Roman circular hall.

The great sense of harmony of the interior is due to its perfect proportions: the diameter is the same as the height, 140 ft., the dome takes exactly half of the height. If you imagine the dome continuing down in its curve, it would form a perfect sphere touching the floor. The Pantheon was achieved thorough a complicated system of relieving arches embedded in the mass of concrete from its foundations to the summit of the dome. The dome was cast as a unique block of cement on a framework with the coffered design on its reserve, using gradually higher building material in successive layers to the summit, while diminishing its thickness from 5.90 meters at the base to 1.50 meters at the top. This dome, entirely built without reinforcement, has been the greatest in the world to this century, (St. Peter's is three ft. less); an engineering feat of the first order which shows the profound knowledge of the techniques of construction required by the intricacy of calculation, which any layman can guess.

Buried in the Pantheon are some of Italy's great artists. There is first of all Raphael; he was also named architect-in-chief on the new St. Peter's at the Vatican by Pope Leo X and was given absolute authority over all monuments, buildings and ruins within a circuit of ten miles around Rome and devoted himself to the study of ancient buildings and ruins (it would not be inappropriate to call him one of the first archeologists in the world). He certainly found in the Pantheon that majestic spirit of the classical world which inspired him and the other great men of the Italian Renaissance. Raphael died at the age of 37, on 6th April 1520, and when he felt the approach of death he expressed the wish to rest in the Pantheon. Over Raphael's grave is the work of his disciple Lorenzetto, the Madonna del Sasso, the Madonna of the Stone. After the unification of Italy, the Pantheon was chosen as the mausoleum for the kings; Vittorio Emanuele II and Umberto I with Queen Margherita di Savoia, his wife, are buried in the smaller apses to the right and left.

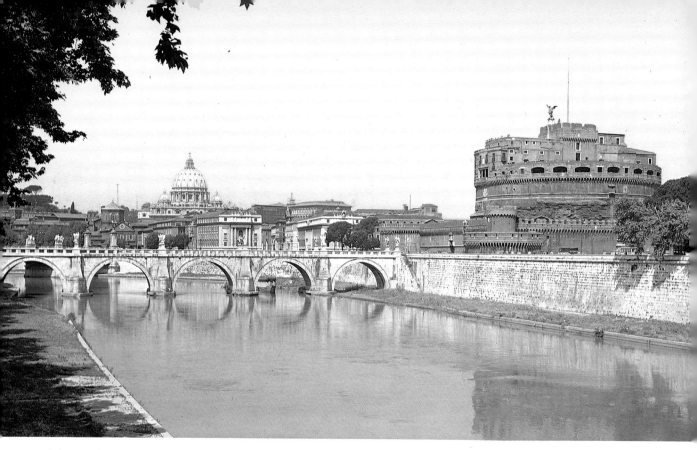

A famous view of Rome: Castel Sant'Angelo, the Bridge of Sant'Angelo, and in the background, St. Peter's.
Reconstruction of Hadrian's mausoleum by G. Gatteschi.

From the Pantheon to St. Peter's

In the fading light of evening, one can see the Tiber and in the distance, St. Peter's dome.

We'il continue across the narrow streets of Campus Martius by the national church of France. **St. Louis of the French**, another artistic treasurehouse church built in the XVI century which contains three precious Caravaggio's: the Calling, the Martyrdom of St. Matthew and St. Matthew with the Angel. Then crossing the Tiber we find ouselves in front of the Palazzo di Giustizia, **the Hall of Justice**, built in 1911 by the architect Calderini; but the great sight is on your left as you cross the river, the **Sant'Angelo Bridge** and **Castel Sant'Angelo** with St. Peter's dome in the far background. The bridge is the one Emperor Hadrian threw across the Tiber as an approach to his huge mausoleum, which he started building in 130 A.D. and which was completed by Antoninus Pius in 139 A.D. The popes made the mausoleum into a fortress and for centuries it was their stronghold. The name of Castel Sant'Angelo is derived from the vision of Pope Gregory I who in 590 led a procession to petition God to stop a plague; while crossing the bridge he saw on top of the fortress the Archangel Michael sheathing a flaming sword, the divine signal that the pestilence was over. (Incidentally, the symptoms of the plague were attacks of sneezing and yawning. When people saw friends yawning and sneezing they made the sign of the cross and said «God bless you», as the Pope had ordered. This habit started on that occasion).

Hadrian's tomb was the mausoleum of the emperors for only sixty years; in 271 it was included in the Aurelian wall, and in 410 it was sacked by the Goths of Alaric. It was first used as a fortress during the siege of Vitigis, another king of the Goths. During the XV and XVI centuries it took on its present appearance; and as it was built as a refuge for the Popes, their apartments were decorated by several of the same artists who worked in the Vatican. If you have some spare time to devote to the exploration of Castel Sant'Angelo, you will find there several works by the disciples of Raphael. This place has also acquired sinister fame as a state prison, you have its parallel in the Tower of London; many visitors will recall Castel Sant'Angelo from the opera La Tosca in which it appears in the third act as a prison.

Leading to St. Peter's Square is the **street of Conciliation**; this new, direct, monumental approach to the Vatican, from Rome, was called Conciliation to commemorate the signing of the Lateran Pact in 1929,

and was inaugurated in 1950 on the occasion of the Jubilee Year.

(With the unification of Italy accomplished in 1861, the Papal State was occupied, and the Pope, Pius IX, refused to deliver the city of Rome to the King. In 1870 on September 20th, Rome was taken over with violence by King Victor Emmanuel II and there were no further diplomatic relations between the Italian State and the Vatican until 1929 when, on February 11th, **the Lateran Pact** was signed and the sovreignties of both the Pope and the Italian King were mutually recognized.)

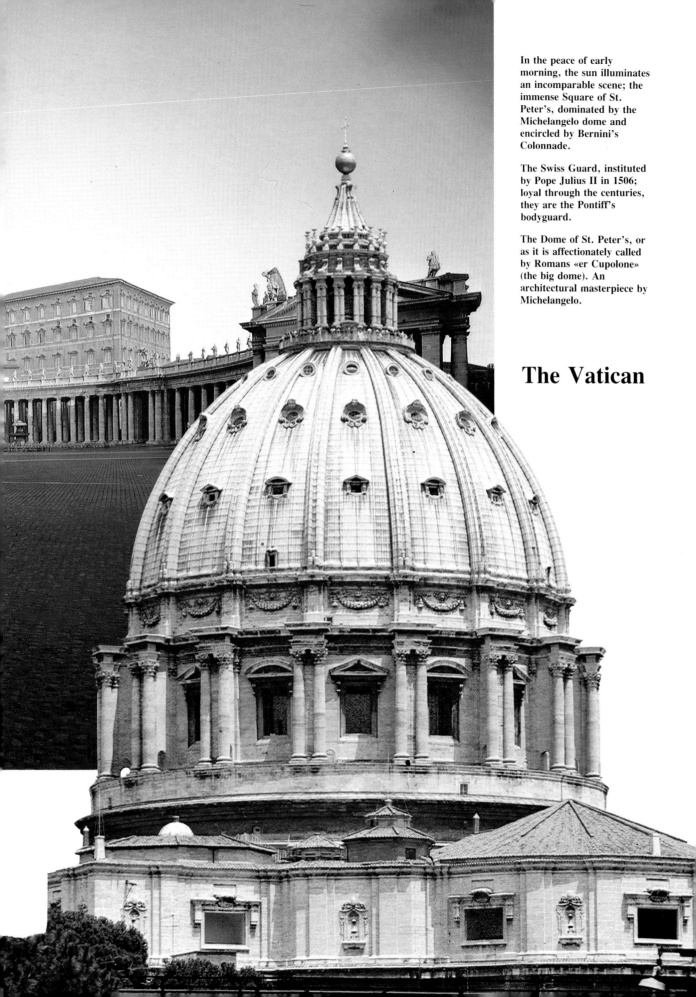

In the peace of early morning, the sun illuminates an incomparable scene; the immense Square of St. Peter's, dominated by the Michelangelo dome and encircled by Bernini's Colonnade.

The Swiss Guard, instituted by Pope Julius II in 1506; loyal through the centuries, they are the Pontiff's bodyguard.

The Dome of St. Peter's, or as it is affectionately called by Romans «er Cupolone» (the big dome). An architectural masterpiece by Michelangelo.

The Vatican

The already famous face of Pope John-Paul II (Wojtyla).

On festival days the immensity of St. Peter's Square is barely sufficient to contain the crowd of pilgrims and visitors from all over the world.

The arms of Pope John Paul II (Wojtyla).

Joannes Paulus PP. II.

St. Peter's Square

At the end of Via della Conciliazione, is Bernini's architectural masterpiece, St. Peter's Square, which can hold over 300,000 people, all embraced by the two immense semicircles of stone, the two long covered walks consisting of 284 columns and surmounted by 142 statues of Saints, all designed by Bernini. This Piazza was built in a short time (between 1655 and 1667) because the architectural project was overseen by Bernini himself. The oldest monument in the square is the monolithic Egyptian obelisk, which stands in the center. Caligula had brought it to Rome to decorate his Circus and near it St. Peter was probably crucified with his head down.

In 1586 under Sixtus V the obelisk was re-erected on its present site and later upon it was placed the emblem of the Chigi Pope Alexander VII, the five small mounts and the star in bronze, this device containing a relic of the Cross. The two beautiful fountains were built at different times; the one on the right by Maderno, in 1615, and the other by Bernini, in 1677, which was the last monument put within the colonnade.

Set into the paving, between the fountains and the obelisk, are two round marble slabs; standing on either of these and observing the colonnade, you have the impression that St. Peter's Square is encircled by a single row of colomns instead of a quadruple one.

Visitors and Romans gather every Sunday on St. Peter's Square for the **Pope's blessing** and particularly on January 1st, Palm Sunday and, of course, on Easter Sunday and Christmas.

Papal Public Audiences are held on Wednesdays in the new Audience Hall or St. Peter's Basilica. During the Pope's summer stay at Castel Gandolfo, the travel companies operate tours to the picturesque region of the Alban Hills including the Papal Audience in his summer residence.

St. Peter's Basilica

Pope Sylvester I, in the year 326 A.D., inaugurated the basilica, built by Emperor Constantine over the grave of St. Peter. The Apostle was martyred in the Circus of Nero in 64 or 67 A.D., and this Circus had always been located where the church stands, until recent excavations proved that St. Peter's foundations were laid on virgin soil. This new fact has posed an archaelogical question to which we do not as yet have the answer. The excavations also proved that the main altar of the church stands right over the grave of St. Peter. During the public audience of June 26th 1968, Pope Paul VI announced that the relics of St. Peter had been identified with consistent archaeological evidence. This was the result of the researches which started in 1939 under Pope Pius XII. The present church was started by Pope Julius II in 1506, and during the 120 years of reconstruction, almost all the major architects of Renaissance contributed in designing and redesigning it.

Bramante was the first, and he also started the ruthless destruction of the old church. The new one he planned in the form of a Greek cross, but both Julius II and Bramante died after a few years, and owing to the political and economic situation of the papacy, the gigantic undertaking didn't make much progress until the 71-year-old **Michelangelo,** in 1546, was named architect-in-chief by Pope Paul III.

Michelangelo's final project was altered by **Della Porta,** who completed the dome, and **Carlo Maderno,** who added the nave and the facade, and at Pope Paul V's command, changed the church into the form of a Latin cross. The new Basilica was consecrated on November 18th, 1626. Through the great central portal, under the **Loggia of Benediction,** from which the newly-elected Pope gives his blessing, we enter the portico with the five doors of the church. The central bronze one was made for the old St. Peter's in 1445 by Filarete from Florence. (If you go to Florence you may compare this with Ghiberti's, made at about the same time.)

At the extreme right is the **Holy Door** which is only opened every 25 years for the Jubilee Year.

When you are finally inside St. Peter's, you cannot at first sight appreciate its magnitude, for your sense of proportion is deceived by the scale of the various parts; you are more and more over-whelmed as you proceed and compare with life-size. A few figures are in any case eloquent; the length including the portico is 690 feet; the vault is 144 ft.; at the far end of the central nave, the dove of the Holy Spirit has a wingspan of five feet. The Church has a standing capacity of 60,000 people. Another idea of its size is given by the brass tablets, on the floor of the central nave, with the comparative length of the greatest cathedrals in the world; second largest is St. Paul's in London.

We begin our tour of the Church with the Chapel of the Pietà, where the finest sculpture of the whole church is kept. **The Pietà** (the Pity) by **Michelangelo,** which he made when he was only 24, represents the sorrow of the Madonna holding Her dead Son and Her acceptance of the will of God. It is the masterpiece of Michelangelo's youth, still under the influence of Florentine sculpture, and is the only statue he ever signed. His name is to be found on the sash across the Madonna's breast (as Michelangelo heard some admirers attributing his work to another artist). The chapel of the Pietà was originally dedicated to the Crucifixion; on the empty cross we read the four letters (**INRI**), standing for Iesus Nazarenus Rex Iudeorum (Jesus of Nazareth, King of the Jews), the inscription put on the Cross to deride Christ. On

St. Peter's Square in the evening, immediately after the election of Pope John Paul I, Luciani, the Pope who reigned for a scarcely a month.

the ceiling above the Pietà is the only fresco painting in the church, the Triumph of the Cross by Lanfranco, XVII century.

All that appears to be painting in St. Peter's is in fact mosaic work, made in the mosaic studio of the Vatican. This is the only place in the world where a painting can be reproduced in mosaic with perfect exactness. They use mainly composition stone.

Continuing along the right aisle and immediately on the right is the **Chapel of the Crucifix,** containing a XII century crucifix, ascribed to Cavallini, and the lift, used by the Pope to enter the church during special ceremonies, or for the weekly public audience on Wednesdays. Opposite the chapel of the Crucifix is the memorial to Christina of Sweden by C. Fontana, one of the few women buried in St. Peter's. She abdicated and converted to Catholicism, which her father, Gustavus Adolphus, had fought against during the Thirty Years War and she came to Rome in 1655. Her grave is in the crypt underneath the church. In the next chapel is a large mosaic reproduction of the Martyrdom of St. Sebastian; the

original painting is by Domenichino, XVII century. In an open glass casket in the altar lies the body of Blessed Innocent XI, who lived in the seventeenth century, his face and his hands are covered with silver. (The title of "Beatus", or "Blessed" is given prior to the declaration of Sainthood).

On the left of it is the fine bronze statue of Pope Pius XII by Messina, 1964. In the same aisle is the **Chapel of the Blessed Sacrament,** a splendid one; above the altar is the gilded bronze pyx by Bernini, who was inspired by the Tempietto di Bramante in the Church of St. Peter's in Montorio. Behind the altar is the only oil-painting in the church, the Trinity by Pietro da Cortona. Beyond the chapel, on the right, is the monument to Pope Gregory XIII, by Rusconi, XVII century, the pope who reformed the old Roman Julian Calendar. There is a relief recalling this event whilich took place in 1582.

As we have now reached the end of the aisle, we return to the central nave and we find ourselves in the part of the Bašilica built by Michelangelo. He had planned the church in the form of a Greek

Cross, the embodiment of the symbol of the Cross, while the immense dome suggests the idea of the sky being inseparable from the Cross. Almost fifty years after Michelangelo had carved the Pietà, for the old St. Peter's, he most reluctantly took in hand his greatest architectural work, which was to be the culmination of his extraordinary life. However, he didn't live to see his dome completed; at the time of his death he had raised it to the height of the drum. Although the alterations and changes by Della Porta and Maderno obscured Michelangelo's original plan, we can still say that this is his greatest work as an architect.

Proceeding to the **High Altar,** on the right and against one of the four immense piers supporting the dome, is the noble statue in bronze of St. Peter enthroned. This is the work of the 13th century Florentine sculptor, Arnolfo di Cambio. (The feet of the statue have been kissed smooth by the faithful). When you stand beneath the vastness of the dome, you see how everything else is dwarfed in sight, even the bronze **canopy by Bernini** which has the height of a five-storey building. We'll note, for instance, that St. Mark's pen, in one of the roundels of the pendentives, is five feet. Beneath the roundels with the mosaic pictures of the four Evangelists are the balconies, decorated with the spiral columns from the canopy of the old St. Peter's, which gave Bernini his idea for the bronze canopy. At Easter the chief relics are exposed from these balconies. They are: the fragment of the Sacred Lance, with which St. Longinus pierced the side of Christ while He was hanging on the Cross, the statue of this Saint, by Bernini, at the base of the pier behind St. Peter's bronze statue; the skull of St. Andrew and his statue in the pier which St. Peter faces; in the other two are the relics of the Cross and Veronica's veil with the statues of St. Helena and St. Veronica.

Underneath the dome and Bernini's canopy, is the main altar, at which only the Pope has the privilege of celebrating Mass, facing the congregation and the rising sun, for the church is orientated facing East like the other major Basilicas, except St. Paul's Outside the Walls. In front of the altar is the lowered part known as **The Confession**, where there is the Kneeling statue of Pope Pius VI by Canova.

Directly beneath the main altar, closed by a gilded grill, is the **Niche of the Pallia,** built in the sixth century, where the Pallium, a long strip-like vestment worn by archbishops during special ceremonies, was placed before being bestowed on the newly-appointed archbishop.

Beyond the canopy is the part of the church used for the most important ceremonies, such as canonizations, beatifications, coronations of the new popes etc. At the end of the nave are two rather conspicuous works by Bernini: the bronze container of **the Cattedra**, the Bishop's chair, held by four Church

St. Peter's. A magnificent view of the central nave.

St. Peter's: Chapel of the Holy Sacrament.

Fathers: St. Ambrose and St. Augustine in front representing the Latin Church, St. Athanasius and St. John Chrysostom, representing the Greek Church; above the Cattedra is the Glory of the Holy Spirit. The other, on the right of the Cattedra, is the monument to Pope Urban VIII.

The young Michelangelo's masterpiece – the Pietà.

The Pietà. On the Madonna's breast you can see the signature of Michelangelo.

The Pietà – detail.

The monument on the left of the Cattedra, of Paul III, is by Guglielmo della Porta. These are two of the finest papal monuments in the church. Encased in Bernini's bronze throne is a wooden chair with ivory ornamentation which according to tradition was the one used by St. Peter. A recent examination of the chair proved this to be the one donated to Pope John VII in 875, by the Carolingian King Charles II the Bald, when he was crowned in St. Peter's on Dec. 25th of that year. It dates from the ninth century.

Crossing the basilica, we traverse the left transept, noting on the right the monument of Alexander VII by Bernini, which was made when he was almost eighty years old, the last work of this indefatigable genius.

Then we come to the **Clementina Chapel** where there is the monument of Pius VII by the Danish sculptor Thorvaldsen, the only monument in the church by a non-catholic artist.

Before entering the left aisle, immediately on the left, is a mosaic reproduction of the **Transfiguration**

by Raphael, his last work which he left unfinished, and which was completed by Giulio Romano, his disciple. The original is in the Pinacoteca, the Vatican picture gallery. Entering the left aisle on the right is the monument to the pope who only reigned 24 days, Leo XI Medici, by Algardi, XVII century. A reference to his very short reign are the roses on the plinth and the words Sic Floruit.

In correspondence to the Chapel of the Blessed Sacrament in the right aisle, closed by the heavy padded leather curtain, is the **Chapel of the Choir,** where the choir of the Julian Chapel sings on Sundays during High Mass. Built into one of the piers on the left is the only papal monument transferred here from the Old St. Peter's, the fine tomb of Pope Innocent VIII by Pollaiolo, dating from the end of the XV century. On a dark plaque of marble at the base of the monument, we read that this Pope witnessed the discovery of the New World. That is incorrect because Pope Innocent VIII died on July 25th, 1492 and Columbus did not sail from Spain until August 3rd. This is, in any case, the first reference to America in St. Peter's.

Facing the monument of Innocent VIII is the statue of **St. Pius X,** the last pope declared a saint, who is buried in the altar of the next chapel in an open glass casket. Built into the next pier on the left is the monument to the last members of the Royal House of Stuart, by Canova: James III (the Old Pretender), Bonnie Prince Charlie, and Henry, Dean of the Cardinals. The reversed torches of the two winged genii allude to the tragedy of this family. Opposite the Stuart monument is the entrance to the dome. Above the door is a mosaic portrait of Clementina Sobieska, the Old Pretender's wife.

The Baptistry is the last chapel, which has a porphyry font, believed to be the cover of Hadrian's sarcophagus in Castel Sant'Angelo. Next we look at the back of the modern bronze door by Giacomo Manzù. This door is mainly dedicated to the Death of Christ and the Death of the Virgin, but on its back is a relief commemorating the Vatican Second Ecumenical Council and Pope John XXIII conversing with Cardinal Rugambwa of Tanganyka.

Having completed the tour of the basilica we go out

Saint Peter's: The tomb of Saint Peter and the Niche of the Pallium.

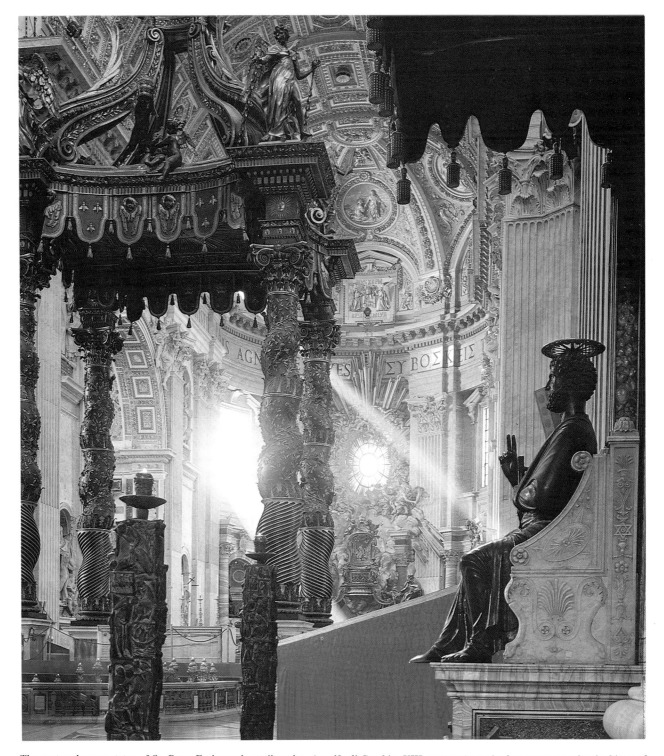

The austere bronze statue of St. Peter Enthroned, attributed to Arnolfo di Cambio, XIII century (note the foot worn away by the kisses of the faithful), is set off by the Baroque splendours of Bernini.

overwhelmed by its stupendous size, and it must be admitted that St. Peter's appears to be overwhelming. We can also understand that Gothic-minded people will find the splendour of gold, mosaics and marble a bit oppressive.

Maybe others will be disappointed to find that this church lacks a sense of Christian humility and simpli-

city — but it must be borne in mind that St. Peter's is the greatest monument to St. Peter and to Christianity. It also is the greatest ceremonial church, and if you are ever fortunate enough to be present in the basilica on one of the great occasions when the Pope is there, you'll see that it really comes into its own. St. Peter's represents the Church Triumphant.

second tour

Vatican Museums and the Sistine Chapel

Our visit this morning will bring us back to the Vatican City, again within the boundary line of the Papal State. Also this part stands over the area which the Etruscans called Vaticus or Mons Vaticus (Vatican hill), one of the places where the Vates, the seers or the prophets, revealed the omens or presages. The side from which we enter the Museums is surrounded by powerful ramparts called Leonine. They were built by Pope Leo IV in 852. In 846, forty-six years after Charlemagne's coronation in St. Peter's, the Saracens descended upon Rome and stripped the fabulous shrines of St. Peter's and St. Paul's, carrying off tons of silver and gold. The plundering lasted one week. After they had gone, Leo IV built a wall around the domain of St. Peter's.

The present entrance to the museum, with the beautiful elliptical double ramp, was built in 1932 by Pope Pius XI. Before that there was a one-mile walk to reach the museum. Above the portal are the modern statues of Michelangelo and Raphael.

The Vatican has been the principal seat of the Popes for about six hundred years. You will recall that the Popes moved to Avignon in 1308 and Gregory XI returned to Rome seventy years later and established his abode in the Vatican, which was another residence of the Bishop of Rome. It was not until the time of Pope Nicholas V that a plan was made for a greatly

enlarged Vatican, to be the most magnificent palace to house the princes of the Church and the myriad treasures accumulated through the centuries. Nicholas V was a great lover of learning and planned, at the same time, to rebuild the Church of St. Peter, which was later started by Julius II.

Guided tours can never afford more than two hours for this visit so we will confine our attention to the most outstanding masterpieces. We will start with the **Hall of the Greek Cross** where there are two magnificent porphyry sarcophagi from the IV century A.D., originally the coffins of St. Helena, mother of Constantine, the one with the battle scenes; the other is of - Constance, the Emperor's daughter. On the floor is a large mosaic from Roman times. **The Round Hall** contains a porphyry bowl in the center, from the ruins of Nero's Golden House. On the floor is a large mosaic work from Otricoli, a place 40 miles from Rome. Also to be found in this room is the head of Jupiter, from Otricoli, ascribed to Briaxis, IV century B.C. and numerous statues of Caesars and pagan gods, the colossal, gilded-bronze statue representing Hercules; and there is Antinous, the favourite of Hadrian.

In the **Hall of the Muses** are the statues of the nine Muses in the Hellenistic style of the III century B.C. from a villa at Tivoli. There are also portraits of personalities from the Greek world, Socrates, Sophocles,

Plato, etc. all copied by the Romans from the original Greek works. There are not many Greek originals in the Vatican; one of the few is the so-called «**Torso Belvedere**». The statue of the Torso bears the signature of a Greek sculptor from Athens, Apollonios, son of Naestor; it is probably part of a fighting figure of Hercules. It was discovered in the ruins of the Baths of Caracalla, and Michelangelo was most impressed by its powerful, perfect anatomy and refused to restore it, as he had been requested to do by the Pope. In the **Room of the Animals** are numerous works from different times, in which animals play a role. There is a copy of the Meleager by Skopas, and the group of Mithras, the Persian god sacrificing the bull to the Sun.

These first three rooms, built by Simonetti, were added by Popes Pius VI and Pius VII in the XVIII and XIX centuries.

Vatican Museum; From above the entrance, one is greeted by statues of Michelangelo and Raphael.

Vatican Museum: The Laocöon.

Courtyard of Belvedere

The octagonal **Courtyard of Belvedere** was the center of the villa, built by Bramante for Pope Innocent VIII at the end of the fifteenth century. In one corner is the **Group of Laocoön;** it was found in the Baths of Titus, near the Colosseum in the XVI century. The sculpture represents the Trojan priest, punished by the gods, for the warning he gave his townsmen about the horse of Troy. The legend says that two serpents came from the sea and killed Laocoön and his two children. This is a remarkable work by Agesandros and his sons, Athenodoros and Polidoros of Rhodes, from the first century B.C. Rhodes was, with Alexandria in Egypt and Ephesus in Turkey, one of the three great centers of art around the Mediterranean during the first century B.C. The art of this period is extremely realistic and the Laocoön group is most representative of it, with the desperate struggle of the priest, in the moment of agony, his muscles exaggera-

From the courtyard of Belvedere to the Stanzas

We are going to omit entirely the other sculpture galleries, and, returning the same way we came, we reach the **Sala della Biga,** (the room of the Chariot), so called from a chariot with two horses, a marble work probably of the II century A.D., reconstructed from ancient fragments. In the same room are copies of Greek statues, the **Discus Thrower** (Discobulus), by Myron, V century B.C. The original was in bronze and does not exist any more; the best copy we have in Rome is the Lancellotti copy, in the Thermae Museum. We cross the **Gallery of the Candelabra,** where you find some more interesting copies of Greek originals, mainly from the Hellenistic period, several urns and coffins from old Roman graves and the beautiful candelabra.

Then we pass into the **Gallery of the Tapestries** which houses a fine collection of original Gobelines, woven in Brussels in the XVI century. The cartoons were drawn by the disciples of Raphael and represent scenes from the life of Christ. On the opposite wall are the tapestries woven in Rome in the XVII century, depicting events from the life of Pope Urban VIII.

The Gallery of the Geographical Maps was decorated by A. Danti in 1581 showing the various districts of Italy and detailed plans and views of Italian cities. The ceiling is by Muziano and his disciples, at the end of the XVI century. We won't spend much time in a couple of rooms containing modern paintings of the XIX century.

In the **Room of the Immaculate Conception** are the frescoes by Podesti, XIX century, commemorating the promulgation of the Dogma of the Immaculate Conception by Pope Pius IX in 1854. There are many real portraits of the clergy.

We enter the Stanze by Raphael.

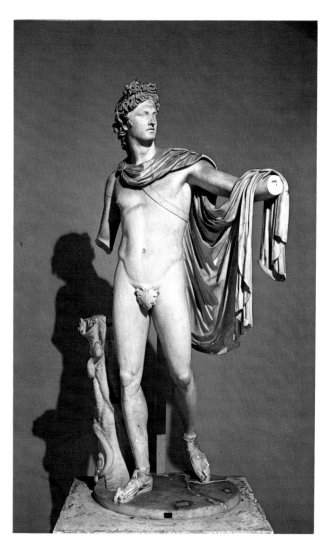

Vatican Museum: The Apollo Belvedere.

tely tense, his sons, one already dying, the other turning his head hopelessly towards his father. Nearby is a plaster copy of the Laocoön, the way you remember it from old pictures, before the first restoration a few years ago was removed, because the right arm of Laocoön was found later proving the restoration to be incorrect. In another corner is the **Apollo Belvedere,** a statue believed to be a copy from a bronze masterpiece by the Greek sculptor Leochares of the IV century B.C. The figure of the god is tall, athletic and slender; he steps forward to see if the arrow he has just thrown has met its mark. Apollo was also the god defender and bringer of peace. This statue was found at Grottaferrata in the fifteenth century.

The Stanzas

The most precious paintings by Raphael are in the apartment built in the XV century for Pope Nicholas V, who was a real humanist, (namely one who in the Renaissance had devoted himself to the rediscovery of ancient philosophies and classic literature, which curch men fought as pagan). Aeneas Silvius Piccolomini of Siena, later elected Pope Pius II, said about Nicholas V «what he does not know is outside the realm of human knowledge». Julius II decided to remodel the apartment and commissioned the work to several eminent painters. Bramante brought Raphael to Rome introducing him to the Pope. Raphael who was only about 25 years old, prevailed over the other artists. Pope Julius let him paint first the ceiling of the room called La Segnatura (the Signature) where the Popes used to sign the Papal bulls and where the Ecclesiastical court of Justice used to hold its audiences. The young artist passed his test brilliantly and the Pope commissioned him to decorate the whole apartment.

The room of the Segnatura he painted in two years, 1509-11; the subjects the Pope suggested, symbolize the elements forming the human spirit, knowledge and virtue; the paintings on the ceiling are in close relation with those on the walls. The Roundel with the figure of Religion corresponds to the **Disputa del Sacramento** (the Disputation of the Sacrament). In this picture we recognize in Raphael the disciple of Perugino, the Umbrian master; the scene is symmetrically divided, the lower part represents Earth and famous theologians are on each side of the altar. The higher section represents Heaven.

The Trinity is centrally situated, starting from the top with God, Christ (sitting with the Virgin Mary, Saints and Prophets) down to The Holy Spirit. On the altar is the vessel containing the Holy Sacrament (the body of Christ), which is the focal point of the whole composition, linking Earth to Heaven according to the Christian faith. Some famous theologians are to be identified in the various figures: popes, Savonarola, Fra' Angelico and Dante Alighieri the poet. The perfect balance and symmetry on which the art of Raphael is based, appears more fluently conceived on the opposite wall, in the painting of **The School of Athens** which refers to the figure of Philosophy on the ceiling. The imposing vaulted structure in the painting, forming the background for the group of the most renowned philosophers, has a floor with such a perfect perspective effect that you could believe it to be a continuation of the floor of this room. The focal point of this composition is in the two central figures: the one in the red mantle, pointing to Heaven is Plato, who represents Idealism; the other in blue, Aristotle, pointing to Earth, represents Reality, the fundamental principles of philosophy. In the numerous group we recognize, in the olive-green robes Socrates; Heraclitus, the pessimist, in the foreground, with the features of Michelangelo. Raphael painted there several portraits; Plato is possibly Leonardo da Vinci. His self-portait is in the group of the philosophers mathematicians, and scientists, on the right corner, where Archimedes, or perhaps Euclid with Bramante's features, draws on a black-board. The self-portrait of Raphael is the face next to the last in the very corner, the beardless young man with a black beret.

Raphael has a fair right to be in that group for, as we see, his art is also made of mathematical precision and perfect equilibrium. Above one of the windows in the lunette are the three virtues relating to the civil and canon law in the scenes below. Over the other window, the Parnassus with Apollo in the center upon a rock, playing his lyre, and the most celebrated poets, Vergil, Homer, Dante etc. are there. This room, more than any other place, is pervaded by the presence of Raphael and of the other great personalities he met there, and we feel the classic atmosphere of the intellectual world which permeated and exhilarated Raphael's alert and versatile genius. The young artist, after having painted for years little else than madonnas and saints, found, in the residence of the Head of the Christian Church, the opportunity of painting pagan subjects. It is a fact that the Vatican Palaces, the seat of Catholic Sovereignty, are also one of the greatest treasure-houses of pagan art.

Under the patronage of humanist popes, the Vatican became the greatest center of culture and art which ever existed in the world. We do not know of any other time in the history of mankind that so many geniuses met in one place. The visitor should bear this in mind when visiting the Vatican. The other face of the coin was the competition between these great

The Belvedere Torso in the Vatican Museum, one of the masterpieces found in the ruins of the Baths of Caracalla.

The Raphael Stanzas: The «Disputation of the Sacrament».

men — a competition which was not always a fair one — being employed by the Pope meant glory and honour, but it also meant money and security. The main contest occurred between tho two greatest men, the two giants, Michelangelo and Raphael. When the latter started decorating the Stanze, Michelangelo had already been painting for a year in the Sistine Chapel. **The room of Heliodorus** was partly painted by Raphael around 1412-14. On the ceiling are scenes from the Bible by B. Peruzzi, on the walls are depicted the subjects which the Pope had chosen to represent the triumph of the Catholic faith. On the back of the wall with the «School of Athens» there is **Leo I meeting Attila, the King of the Huns.**

The Pope has the features of Pope Leo X (Julius II did not live to see this room finished and he was succeeded by Leo X Medici). This picture is by the assistants of Raphael and we notice that the figures in it are almost out of proportion in comparison with the perfection of the School of Athens. On the opposite wall, by Raphael, is Heliodorus expelled from the Temple of Jerusalem, where he had stolen the treasure, by order of Seleucus Philopator. It is a clear allusion to the expulsion of the French from Italy. On the left Pope Julius II on his portable throne, wearing the beard he grew when he started the crusade against the French; he swore he would not remove it until he had cast them out of Italy. The interesting study of gleaming light in this picture presages the fine example of luminarism Raphael achieved in the **Liberation of St. Peter**, over one of the windows.

Over the opposite window is the **Miracle of Bolsena**. While a Bohemian priest, doubting the doctrine of Trans-substantiation, was celebrating Mass at Bolsena, near Orvieto, the Host dripped blood. The miracle is connected with the celebration of Corpus Domini in June.

Pope Julius II is portrayed on the right of the altar confronting the priest of the miracle who shows dismay and uncertainty. Behind him anxiety appears on

Raphael Stanzas: The School of Athens.

the faces of the people. On the priest's side wind blows on the candles, but the candles burn quietly on the Pope's side. There is certainty of faith, trust and calm.

In this picture we notice a remarkable study of color (the Venetian Sebastiano del Piombo was also in the Vatican then), with its predominant red tones.

So many other works were commissioned from Raphael, that he had to employ a whole school of assistants, whom he lodged in his princely house, never tiring of giving personal supervision to their studies, their works and their welfare. The **Room of Costantine**, entirely by the disciples of Raphael, was completed in 1525, five yars after his death. Giulio Romano painted the battle of the Milvian Bridge and the Vision of Constantine, Francesco Penni the Baptism of Constantine and the Donations. The ceiling of this room was painted in 1585 by Laureti. **The Loggias** overlooking the Courtyard of San Damaso were designed by Bramante at the end of the XV century, and

all are decorated with frescoes by Raphael and his assistants in the style called Grotesque. This type of decoration was discovered by the Renaissance artists in the remains of the old Roman Imperial palaces and the Domus Aurea, places which the Romans called grottoes. On the ceiling are scenes from The Bible.

Returning thorough the rooms we have seen, we'll stop in the **Stanza dell'Incendio di Borgo** (Fire in the Borgo) which is the last work in the Stanze by Raphael himself, but only in part. The scene represents the fire in the district near St. Peter's put out by miracle when Pope Leo IV bestowed his blessing. In this painting we notice another change in Raphael's style, who felt considerably the influence of Michelangelo's powerful personality. The strongly built figures, the study of anatomy and many details in some movements remind us of Michelangelo's art.

We leave the Stanze, where the Cardinals live during the **Conclave** (the election of the Pope), and we go to the Sistine Chapel.

Raphael Stanzas: The
Deliverance of St. Peter;
detail

Raphael Stanzas: School of
Athens, detail; Plato and
Aristotle, in the Stanza della
Segnatura).

Raphael Stanzas: Self portrait
of Raphael and portrait of
Sodoma, detail from the
School of Athens.

The Sistine Chapel

The Sistine Chapel was built by Giovannino de' Dolci for Pope Sixtus IV, in 1473. Sixtus IV is the Pontiff who also built the Sistine Bridge (Ponte Sisto) over the Tiber, is the founder of the Sistine Choir, and one of the Popes who developed into greatness the Vatican Library.

The Chapel was named after him, and was intended for the most important ceremonies. It is in this Chapel that the Cardinals sit in Conclave to elect the new Pope. Its architecture is very simple, a great hall-shaped building (43 metres long, 13 metres wide and 26 metres high). A wonderful marble screen by Mino da Fiesole, XV century, divides the chapel; one section, the larger one, is reserved for the clergy, the other for the congregation. The floor in the opus Alexandrinum echoes the mediaeval Cosmatesque art; the paintings engage our attention — on them more has been written perhaps than on any other work of art in the whole world. The decoration of the chapel reflects the Mediaeval conception, according to which the world was divided into three epochs: the first,

before God gave the Laws to Moses; the second, after the Laws were given to Moses and the third, the period of grace starting with the Birth of Christ.

The two side walls were painted first. On one side are the panels with the **Life of Moses**, on the other the **Life of Christ. The Old** and **The New Testament.** These frescoes were executed by eminent Florentine and Umbrian painters. Starting from the Last Judgement, the scenes from the **Life of Moses** are as follows: Moses and his wife in Egypt; the Circumcision of their Son, by Pinturicchio and his pupils; the Burning Bush, Moses killing the Egyptian and Driving the Midianites from the fountain, Jethro's daughters by Botticelli; Pharaoh drowned in the Red Sea, painted by Domenico Rosselli or Ghirlandaio; Moses on Mt. Sinai and the Golden Calf by Cosimo Rosselli; the Punishment of Korah, Dathan and Abiram by Botticelli; Moses giving the Rod to Joshua and the Death of Moses, by Luca Signorelli and Bartolomeo della Gatta. The panels with the **Life of Christ** on the other wall represent: the Baptism of Christ, by Pinturicchio

Solemn ceremony in the Sistine Chapel;
lithograph by Benoist, 19th century.

ENIA PONTES:
VAM
MODA PORTVS:

Pope Sixtus IV and his nephew, Cardinal Giuliano della Rovere,
who later became Pope Julius II. Detail of the painting by Melozzo
da Forlì «Sixtus IV with Platina», Vatican Picture Gallery.

The marvellous self portrait of Michelangelo from the house of
Buonarroti in Florence.

or Perugino; the Temptation by Botticelli; the Calling of St. Peter and St. Andrew, by Domenico del Ghirlandaio; the Sermon on the Mount, by Cosimo Rosselli and Piero di Cosimo; the Consignment of the Keys, by Perugino; the Last Supper by Cosimo Rosselli.

For two years these prominent artists worked side by side to paint the chapel; for two years each of them endeavoured to produce his masterpiece. The decoration was accomplished between 1480-82.

Vatican Museums. The Sistine Chapel.

The Sistine Chapel: the vault. From «The Division of Light and Darkness» to «The Creation of Woman».

The Sistine Chapel; From «The Creation of Woman» to «The Drunkenness of Noah».

The Ceiling

It is because of Michelangelo's work that most visitors go to the Sistine Chapel. It is his work that rivets our attention to the exclusion of all others. Visiting St. Peter in Chains we shall see how Michelangelo had to interrupt the mausoleum of Julius II, and returned to Florence after a quarrel with the Pope. Later they were reconciled and he came back to Rome again in great favour by the Pope and hoping to complete the mausoleum. To his astonishiment the Pope commissioned him to paint the fresco decoration of this ceiling, which at that time was painted only with gold stars against a blue back-ground. Michelangelo did all he could to evade the commission, protesting that he knew nothing of fresco painting but the Pope persisted and he had to yield. It is said that Bramante, the fellowtownsman of Raphael and a bitter rival of Michelangelo, persuaded Pope Julius II to let Michelangelo paint the ceiling of the Chapel, in the belief that he would either refuse or fail as a painter. It was the competition which caused him to paint in the Sistine Chapel.

The Pope only wanted Michelangelo to paint the twelve Apostles in the lunettes and a decorative design on the ceiling; but Michelangelo proposed then to paint the whole ceiling and Julius II gave his assent. He started painting on May 10th 1508, and it took him four years to complete this titanic work, four years of indescribable fatigue and of stormy relations with the Pope. One day, tired of waiting for the work to be finished, at a rude reply from Michelange-

lo, Julius II struck him with his stick, after which the artist rushed home to prepare to leave for Florence, but the Pope sent his apologies and two hundred ducats, which Michelangelo accepted. On All Saints Day 1512 the paintings were uncovered, eliciting a universal chorus of praise. Three and a half months later Pope Julius II died. Michelangelo then went back to Florence. The scenes Michelangelo painted on the ceiling are framed by the painted cornices; he painted first and architectural structure, and divided the ceiling in its length into three bands; in the central one he depicted **Genesis**, from the Separation of Light from Darkness to the Drunkness of Noah: all around, above the side walls in the triangular spaces and in the lunettes, are the ancestors of Christ, David's line; alternately on the spandrels between them are prophets and sibyls. In the triangular spaces in the corners of the Chapel are the four miraculous salvations of the Hebrews: David and Goliath, Judith and Holophernes, the Crucifixion of Amman and the Brazen Serpent.

Already at the first glimpse of this tremendous vision the visitor realizes that Michelangelo in this chapel achieved something more than human. He will also realize that the innumerable descriptions and the much picturing are not enough to prepare one for the impact which it makes, and, to be frank, we may at the first feel a sense of disconcert. The time we spend in the Sistine Chapel is much too short, it will be difficult to immediately find the key to the understan-

ding of Michelangelo's spirit and certainly many people left the Chapel wondering what really determines the importance of these paintings, why more has been written on them than possibly any other work of art in the world.

In order not to leave the chapel asking ourselves the same questions, we must try to see these works in perspective with their age and consider something which everyone can see: the striking contrast between the paintings of the side walls and the ones by Michelangelo. It is this difference of two totally different strains of thought, produced by the same epoch, which provides a ready access to the artistic history of the Chapel and the key to the understanding of Michelangelo's spirit.

The paintings on the side walls hark back to the mediaeval concepts of life; they are still based on the mystical relationship which lay at the foundation of mediaeval life; they are still bound by the moral ideals involved in ascetism, scholasticism and the poverty of the Creature. Although at the end of XV

century, the intellectual activity, the revival of art and culture, the rediscovery of ancient philosophies, the scientific and geographical discoveries (the discovery of America), the invention of the press and so forth, had opened new ways for human development, (it was in the XV century that the world started moving faster), artists of the calibre of Botticelli and Perugino, when commissioned a painting by the Church were given a detailed description of the painting required; they would not dare to add anything of their own invention and they worked on a severe scheme (hard to recognise the Botticelli we know from Florence paintings: «The Birth of Venus» and «The Spring»). The result is that to the layman the side wall paintings look more or less alike. The figures depicted by Michelangelo were inspired by the dignity of man, by Plato's philosphy («the perfect man in the perfect state»), he broke thorough the bonds of mediaeval traditionalism, his human figures are perfect in thair anatomy, strongly built and express intelligence; they are freed from their heavy mantles, as they are freed from mediaeval presuppositions and in them we finally see freedom of creation. (Michelangelo's two greatest loves were sculpture and freedom).

In his figures Michelangelo represented the precious gifts God gave Man, showing another dimension of the human race with the awareness of the possibilities and the abilities Man has to build his own world, to build his own future. Let us put it into modern language: Man who was to walk on the Moon.

Sistine Chapel: Detail from «The Creation of Man» by Michelangelo.

The Final Judgement

Michelangelo started the decoration of the end wall, twenty-two years after he had painted the ceiling, summoned to Rome by Pope Paul III. **The Last Judgement** represents seven years of work. Michelangelo was in his sixties; during those years away from Rome his life had been deeply embittered and most of the works he had started he left unifinished. He had lost his father, whom he loved immensely; he had lost his favourite brother; he had lost his health and his faith in his fatherland. Rome had just experienced the most ferocious sacking of her history under Charles V, which people saw as a manifestation of the wrath of God; the Reformation of the Church and a movement for spiritual regeneration followed. The drama of this historical moment and of Michelangelo's life are reflected in the turmoil of the almost three hundred figures which he painted in

Sistine Chapel; The Delphic Sibyl, by Michelangelo.

Sistine Chapel; The Last Judgement.

Sistine Chapel; Detail, of The Last Judgement.

Sistine Chapel; The Last Judgement; Self portrait of Michelangelo on the skin of St. Bartholomew.

the Last Judgement. These figures were entirely naked and this aroused violent criticism. Michelangelo was accused of Lutheranism (the Inquisition was incubating); the master of ceremonies of the Vatican, a Cardinal, declared the figures obscene; Michelangelo retorted by painting the Cardinal's portrait in Hell, with the ears of an ass and a serpent around his loins, to represent Minos. (The extreme bottom right hand corner). After the death of Pope Paul III, the figures were partly covered, Daniele da Volterra was the painter who executed the order and who was known ever after as «Il Braghettone» (the breeches maker).

The gigantic Christ, the inexorable judge, was criticised for being represented as a beardless young man. Around Christ and the Virgin Mary, are the martyrs, showing the symbols of their martyrdom; the face on the skin of St. Bartholomew, the Saint skinned alive (below Christ, to the right when you look at the picture), is the tragic mask of Michelangelo; the distorted face shows all his bitterness and alludes to all the wrongs done to him.

We find many more portraits in this picture, and a lot of details of interest. In the center are the angels blowing the trumpets to awaken the dead, represented at the bottom (in the left hand corner).

Other angels raise the elect to Heaven. We'll note the mighty angel raising, by means of a string of rosary beads, two colored men who deserved preservation because of their attention to work as well as faith. On the section to the right are the rebellious damned, pulled down to Hell. Beyond this screen of drama, we find the conception which had been the main concern of a Renaissance humanist «that a proper study of mankind, is Man»; in the end it is the human figure which dominates in these frescoes (you hardly see any landscape).

The paintings on the ceiling were the culmination of what had been done before in painting; and they are in painting what St. Peter's is in architecture: the crowing achievement of the revival of learning. The Last Judgement sealed the whole epoch. Michelangelo with these paintings said the last word about the Renaissance; symbolising all the newness, the freshness, the renovation and the innovations of this age. The paintings of the Sistine Chapel, more than any other work suggest parallelisms, with current events of our age, and provide a link between Michelangelo's world and our own. In this, may be, we find the explanation for the great appeal that his art had to the men of all time.

The Library

Having reached the supreme work, as it were, of the whole Vatican Museum, it seems an anticlimax to try to describe anything else. On the way out we'll see the **Sancta Sanctorum**, containing most precious relics (from the Lateran) and in one room part of **the Treasury,** consisting mainly of presents to the Church from all parts of the world; note the fine ivories and enamels from Limoges. Contained in the **Christian Museum** are gold-painted glasses and bronze lamps from the Catacombs. Rather hurriedly we pass through **the Sistine Hall,** completed in 1588, by Sixtus V which is two hundred and twenty feet long; we'll note the contents, at least some of them, in the glass cases: the Vatican Codex B, the Gutemberg Bible, the autographed letters of Raphael, Michelangelo, Martin Luther, Galileo and two love letters from Henry VIII to Anne Boleyn, thereby losing the title of Defender of the Faith, conferred to him by the Pope for his book on the Sacraments. It was Nicolas V who was the real founder of the Vatican Library; when he was elected, there were in the Vatican 340 books, when he died there were 1200. He employed hundreds of scholars and copyists.

We leave the Museum and you are recommended to make a return visit to see the Pinacoteca (the Picture Gallery of the Vatican), which has the advantage of not being large, but it contains Raphael's great picture of the Transfiguration and his Madonna di Foligno. Besides, you may be interested in visiting the Etruscan Museum, the Egyptian collection and the historically and artistically most interesting Borgia Apartment, decorated by Pinturicchio, where there are several portraits of the Borgia and Farnese families.

Vatican Museum: The Sistine Room in the Library.

Vatican Picture Gallery. The Transfiguration by Raphael.

Piazza della Repubblica.
Detail of the Fountain of the
Naiads and view of the
Basilica of St. Mary of the
Angels.

Museum of the Baths of
Diocletian (Terme Museum):
The three bas-reliefs from
the so called Ludovisi
Throne, Greek original, 5th
century BC, one of the most
famous masterpieces
contained in the museum.
The figures represent:
centre, the Birth of Venus;
left, the bride and the
Hetaera on the right.

Terme Museum: The Discus Thrower of Myron, 5th century BC (from Castel Porziano).

Terme Museum; The Cyrene Venus.

Piazza della Repubblica is better know as Piazza Esedra because of its shape, which retraces the architectural shape of the ancient exedra of the Baths of Diocletian. On the site of this monument there now stands the fine fountain of the Naiads, the work of the sculptor Rutelli, inaugurated in 1901.

On one side of this piazza stand the remains of the largest Baths built during the whole Roman Empire — the Baths of Diocletian, which were completed in 305 A.D. In the sixteenth century, Michelangelo transformed the «tepidarium» (the chamber in which the water was kept at a tepid temperature) into the Church of Santa Maria degli Angeli. The rest of the Baths is taken up by the Roman National Museum, or «Museo delle Terme», where sculpture of the greatest interest and well-known masterpieces of the Greek and Roman artists can be found.

A few yards away from Piazza della Repubblica is the busy cross-roads of the Largo Santa Susanna, together with Piazza San Bernardo which stands next to it. The church of Santa Susanna was originally built in the eighth century on the site of the saint's martyrdom, and after a number or restorations, a fine façade by Carlo Maderno was completed at the beginning of the seventeenth century. The Church is now the national church of American Catholics in Rome.

The Church of San Bernardo was built by converting a round building from the Baths of Diocletian, at the end of the sixteenth century.

On one side of Largo Santa Susanna stands the picturesque Moses Fountain, the work of Domenico Fontana in the sixteenth century. It was built to celebrate the restoration of the Acqueduct of the Acqua Felice, under Pope Sixtus V. The huge and much-criticised statue of Moses was traditionally ascribed to Prospero da Brescia, but in fact it is the work of L. Sormani.

On the corner made by Largo Santa Susanna and Via Venti Settembre stands the Church of Santa Maria della Vittoria, by Carlo Maderno. It was rededicated to the Madonna to celebrate the victory of the catholic army over the armies of Frederick of Bohemia, the Elector Palatine, at Prague in 1620. This church, however, owes its fame principally to another great masterpiece by Bernini — «Saint Teresa overwhelmed by the Love of God», better known as «Saint Teresa in Ecstasy».

Largo di Santa Susanna

The Quirinal

After travelling down Via Venti Settembre and Via del Quirinale, we arrive at Piazza del Quirinale, and from the balcony standing at the crown of its hill we can enjoy a fine panorama through the gap, with the dome of S. Peter's in the background. The Quirinale is the highest of the seven hills of Rome, and in ancient times it was dedicated to the God Quirinus (the hill was occupied by Sabines who came from the city of Curi). The palace of the Quirinale, built by the Popes in the second half of the sixteenth century, was their summer residence until 1870. It then became the royal palace until 1947, and now it is the official residence of the President of the Republic.

At the centre of the piazza which stands before the palace is the **Fountain of Castor and Pollux** with four old Roman statues of the twin gods and the horses, possibly copies from Greek originals, found near the Baths of Constantine on the Quirinal hill. In 1787 was added the obelisk from the Mausoleum of Augustus, and in 1818 the basin in grey granite from the Forum where it once was in front of the Curia. Soon after the Quirinale we arrive at the Trevi Fountain.

Piazza del Quirinale. Quirinale Palace and Castor and Pollux Fountain.

Piazza del Quirinale; detail of the fountain of Castor and Pollux.

Quirinale Palace. «The Corazzieri» – the bodyguard of the President of the Republic in one of the palace state-rooms.

Trevi Fountain

The historian Pliny had included in the wonders of the ancient world, the acqueducts of Rome, known as Regina Aquarum, the Queen of Waters. In fact Rome had the most wonderful monumental fountains. During the Empire, when Rome had about one and a half million inhabitants, the city was supplied with water by fourteen large acqueducts. At the fall of the Empire, Rome was besieged and sacked, and to cut the water supply the acqueducts were all destroyed or seriously damaged, and all through the middle ages the Romans suffered from shortage of water. During the Renaissance the Popes restored some of the acqueducts, and, it was mainly to celebrate the return of water that the famous monumental fountains were built; again Rome is the city of fountains. The most celebrated of them, at least the most renowned, from pictures, is the fountain of Trevi. The fountain we see now was completed in 1762 and was designed by Nicola Salvi.

It took thirty years to build and construction was not begun until two centuries after plans had been made for this big fountain. This very spectacular fountain is also the last important monumental work in Rome in the Baroque style. It represents the triumph of Oceanus riding through a triumphal arch on a seashell pulled by tritons and two seahorses, one tamed and one untamed, to symbolise calm and rough waters. The four woman's figures up above represent the seasons of the year. The water supplying this fountain is called the Virgin Water. On one of the bas-reliefs on the fountain, you read the legend of the Roman maiden showing the source of this spring to a group of thirsty Roman soldiers coming from battle.

The first Trevi acqueduct was built under Augustus Caesar by Consul Agrippa, the same who built the first Pantheon. Tradition goes that before you leave Rome, you should cast a coin into this fountain to ensure your return. Trevi fountain is very pretty at night when it is floodlit, and it is also very centrally located, only two blocks from Via del Corso and one block from Via del Tritone.

Continuing from the Trevi Fountain to Piazza Venezia, you cross **Via del Corso,** which is the main street of Rome. In all Italian cities and towns there is a via del Corso, the central street where they used to hold, in the Middle Ages and the Renaissance, the Corse (horse races). On Via del Corso you still see several old patrician palaces, most of them made into banks or office buildings. Before you enter Piazza Venezia, the palace next to the last on your right, is the **Doria Palace,** still privately owned by that family, the palace being known as the most magnificent private palace in Europe. There is also a most interesting private art collection which can be visited on certain days. The

pearl of the collection is the famous portrait of the Pamphilij Pope, Innocent X, by Velasquez.

Piazza Venezia is the center of all national celebrations in Rome; its much criticised **memorial to Victor Emmanuel II** is dedicated to the independence of our Country. It was inaugurated in 1911, designed by Sacconi, built all in white marble from Botticino, near Brescia in northern Italy, and took 26 years to build.

In the center of the monument is the equestrian statue of Victor Emmanuel II, the king who ruled Italy after the unification, and underneath the statue is the tomb of the Unknown Soldier of the First World War. Facing the monument, on your right, is the historical **Palazzo Venezia,** the Palace of Venice, an early Renaissance building exactly 500 years old. Mussolini had his headquarters there, and from the little central balcony he made his famous speeches. The palace is now a museum. The oldest monument in the square is on the left of the big memorial, the valuable Greek marble **column of Emperor Trajan,** erected in 110 A.D. to celebrate the victories of Trajan over the Dacians.

After taking pictures of Piazza Venezia and skirting the Palace of Venice, we go to the right of the Victor Emmanuel monument and we arrive in front of the two staircases leading to **the Capitol.** The steeply ri-

Piazza Venezia

Piazza Venezia; monument to Victor Emanuel II, and the ruins of the Basilica Ulpia.

Trajan's Column.

Piazza Venezia; Venezia Palace and the piazza on Republic Day, 2 June.

Interior of the Synagogue.

The Theatre of Marcellus and the ruins of Apollo Sosiano Temple.

sing one, built over the ruins of an aparment house from the third century A.D., leads to St. Maria of Aracoeli, a mediaeval church; the other, gently sloping and surmounted by the statues of Castor and Pollux, leads to the Capitoline Square; it was designed by Michelangelo and called the **Cordonata.** On the right is via del Teatro di Marcello.

If you continue along via del Teatro di Marcello, you see, straight ahead of you the remains of **Marcellus' Theater** started by Julius Caesar and completed by Augustus (it had a seating capacity of 10,000 people) and to the right of it three columns of the **Temple of Apollo Sosiano,** built in the second century after Christ. Over the remains of Marcellus' theater the Orsini family built a palace, in the 16th century. You will also see two small, well-preserved temples built about two thousand years ago. They are the **temple of Fortuna Virilis**, the rectangular one built in Ionic style, and the circular one called the **Vesta temple**.

Beyond these two temples soars the lofty, XIII century, Romanesque belfry of **Santa Maria in Cosmedin;** the finest mediaeval belfry in Rome. We come immediately in sight of the **Tiber island** with the two old Roman bridges. The oldest one is the Fabricius bridge, built in 64 B.C. Horatius's bridge was also near here. Turning away from the island, on your left, stands the **Synagogue,** rebuilt in 1904 in the Jewish quarter, in the Assyrian-Babylonian style.

Marcellus' Theater

The Jewish quarter and the Synagogue, seen from the Campidoglio. In the foreground three columns from the Temple of Apollo by Sosius.

The Tiber Island and Fabrician Bridge, 62 BC.

The Tiber Island
and Piazza
Bocca della Verità

The Church of Santa Maria in Cosmedin.

Piazza Bocca della Verità (Mouth of Truth). The circular so-called Temple of Vesta and the Temple of Portunus, better known as the Temple of Fortuna Virilis, from the Republican era.

Santa Maria in Cosmedin: The «Bocca della Verità» or «Mouth of Truth». This is an ancient marble mask of a river god, which once served as a cover. The legend has it that the mouth would bite the hand of anyone not telling the truth.

Tiber Island seen from the south with the Cestian Bridge to the left and Fabrician Bridge to the right. In the foreground, the ruins of the Emilian Bridge («Ponte Rotto» – Broken Bridge).

The Capitol

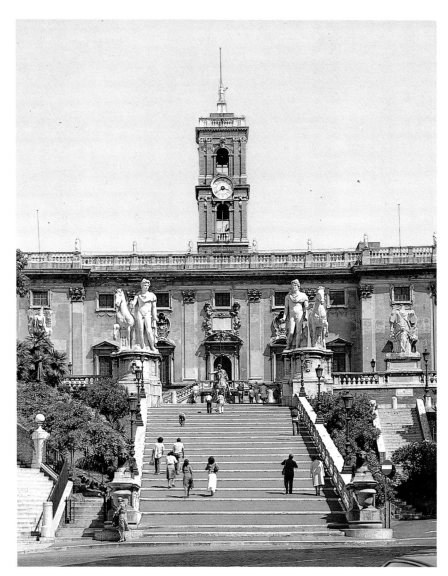

The Campidoglio. «La Cordonata» steps by Michelangelo.

Reconstruction of the Temple of Jupiter, by G. Gatteschi.

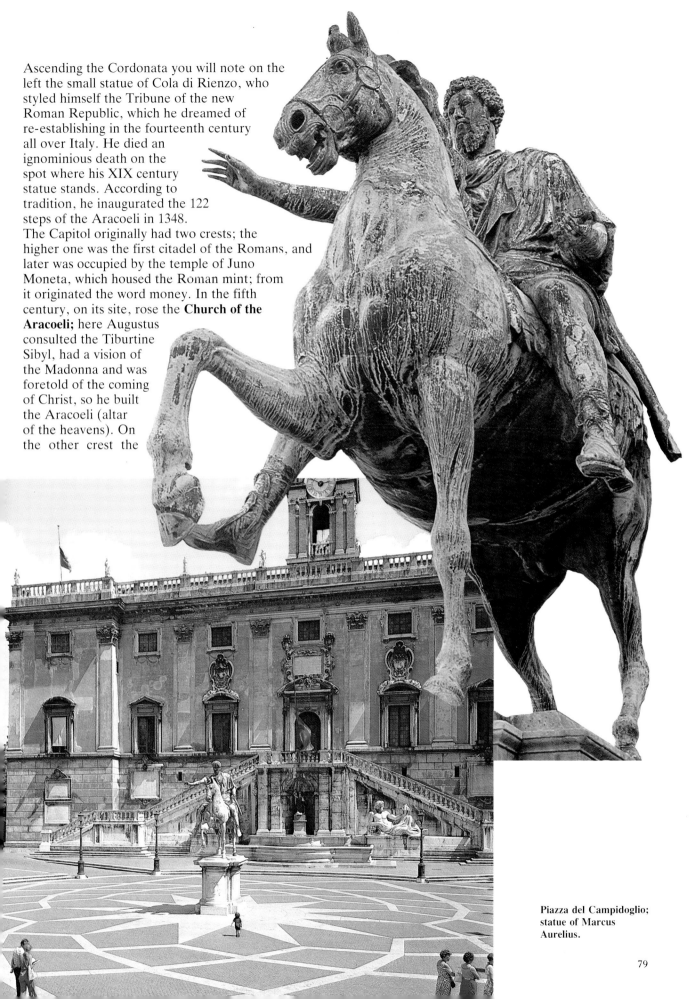

Ascending the Cordonata you will note on the left the small statue of Cola di Rienzo, who styled himself the Tribune of the new Roman Republic, which he dreamed of re-establishing in the fourteenth century all over Italy. He died an ignominious death on the spot where his XIX century statue stands. According to tradition, he inaugurated the 122 steps of the Aracoeli in 1348.

The Capitol originally had two crests; the higher one was the first citadel of the Romans, and later was occupied by the temple of Juno Moneta, which housed the Roman mint; from it originated the word money. In the fifth century, on its site, rose the **Church of the Aracoeli;** here Augustus consulted the Tiburtine Sibyl, had a vision of the Madonna and was foretold of the coming of Christ, so he built the Aracoeli (altar of the heavens). On the other crest the

Piazza del Campidoglio; statue of Marcus Aurelius.

79

temple of Jupiter was built in 510 B.C. It was the most important of the pagan sanctuaries, and with the 24 or 25 more temples built around it, the Capitol became the center of the Roman religious life, and the culminating point for triumphs. Between the crests was a hallowed spot (more or less the site occupied by the present square) so that, facing the Town Hall, the central building in the square, the temple of Jupiter was on the right.

In the middle ages the **Senator's Palace (Town Hall)** was built as the meeting place for senators, elected after an uprising against the government of the popes in 1143; but the Senate was not recognized, and from

1358 only one Senator was appointed by the Pope, which explains the singular Senator. This institution lasted until the unification of Italy. Now the palace is the office of the Mayor of Rome. In mediaeval times this square was also used as a market place and as a place for executions. The Renaissance facade of the Senator's Palace is the work of Girolamo Rainaldi and Giacomo della Porta, XVI century. The square, as we see it now, was planned by Michelangelo in 1538 for the arrival in Rome of Emperor Charles V, who, for his victories over the infidels, was granted a triumphal procession across the Forum and the Capi-

Bronze male bust of the third century BC, known as a portrait of «Junius Brutus».

The Palace of the Conservatori. Spinario Room.

«Boy with a thorn». Beautiful sculpture in bronze – 1st century BC, Hellenic influence.

tol, in the style of the old Roman Emperors, but it was not finished until a century later. When Charles V arrived they had advanced as far as erecting the riding **statue of Marcus Aurelius,** the most famous equestrian monument of the ancient world. It originally stood near the Lateran and was believed to represent Constantine and that explains how it escaped from the turmoil of religious vandalism. The buildings on each side of the square, house the first public collection of classic sculpture in the world. **The palazzo dei Conservatori,** on the right, has among the other famous masterpieces, the bronze **She-Wolf,** and the

Boy with the Thorn. In the court-yard are the remains of a colossal statue of Constantine and a mutilated inscription with the word **BRIT,** the first four letters of the word Britannia; it is a fragment of the arch of Claudius, erected to celebrate his conquest of Britain. He was the first Roman Emperor to tread English soil, and this is the oldest reference to Britain existing in Rome. **The Capitoline Museum,** on the left, has the most complete collection of portraits of Roman Emperors and the famous **dying Gaul.** Beyond the Senator's Palace is the best vantage point from which to look at the Forum.

Capitoline Museum. The Dying Gaul. School of Pergamo, 1st century BC.

Conservatory Museum. The Esquiline Venus, 1st century BC.

Piazza del Campidoglio (Capitol square) seen from above. One of ▶ the perspectives of this Piazza as planned by Michelangelo.

Capitoline Museum. Portrait of a woman, 1st century BC.

The Forum

From there you discover that the City Hall rose over mediaeval buildings (still visible are the towers at the corners) which in turn had been built upon the **Tabularium,** the Records Office, where the Tabulae (the Tablets) were kept. It was built by Sulla in 78 B.C. This is also the precipitous face of the Capitol, commonly known as the **Rock of Tarpeia,** the girl who betrayed the Citadel to the Sabines and was killed by them. The traitors of Rome were executed by being hurled from the summit of the Rock.

At the foot the Capitol, where the Clivus Capitolinus begins, (the rising Roman street with the original paving still on the site) we notice the remains of three temples. They are: the **Porticus Deorum Consentium,**

The Roman Forum and the Colosseum in an evocative night picture.

Roman Forum. View from south, towards the Capitol. At the right the Arch of Septimius Severus and at the left the remains of the Temple of Saturn. In the center the Column of Phocas and the three columns of the Temple of Vespasian. In the background the Palazzo Senatorio which rests on the ruins of the Tabularium.

The so-called tomb of Romulus.

The Forum, as it is today.

A Reconstruction of the Roman Forum. In the foreground at the left stand the Curia, the Arch of Septimius Severus, the Rostra, the Column of Phocas and the Temple of Saturn. In the middle-ground are the Basilica Aemilia on the left and the Basilica Julia on the right. Further back at the left are the Temple of Antoninus and Faustina, the Temple of Julius Caesar Deified, the little circular Temple of Vesta and the Temple of Castor and Pollux. In the background, at the left is the Colosseum behind the Basilica of Maxentius and the Temple of Venus and Rome; at the right are the Imperial Palaces.

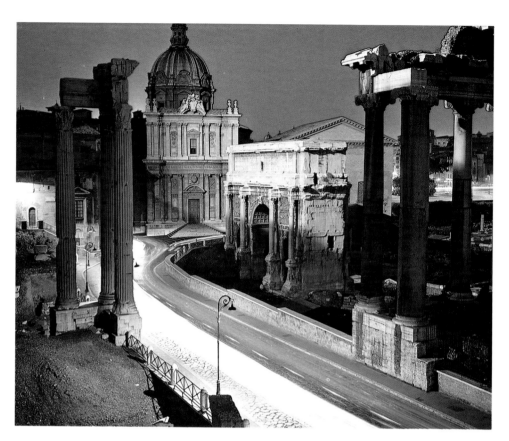

Roman Forum. Arch of Septimius Severus, church of Saints Luke and Martina and a glimpse of the Curia at night.

The same area as shown to us by Piranesi in a beautiful engraving of the 18th century, before the excavations were started.

This beautiful panoramic view of the Roman Forum, seen from the Capitol in an engraving by G. Vasi is of the same period.

Arco di Settimio Severo

Palestrina   la Colonna   M. Compatri   Frascati   Grotta ferrata   Rocca di Papa   Marino   Castel Gandolfo   Albano
  Zagarolo   M. Porcio

ROMA QVANTA FVIT   IPSA RVINA DOCET

Le Rovine delle antiche magnificenze di Roma che si veggono nel Campo Vaccino.   Da Giuseppe Vasi disegnato e inciso l'anno 1771.

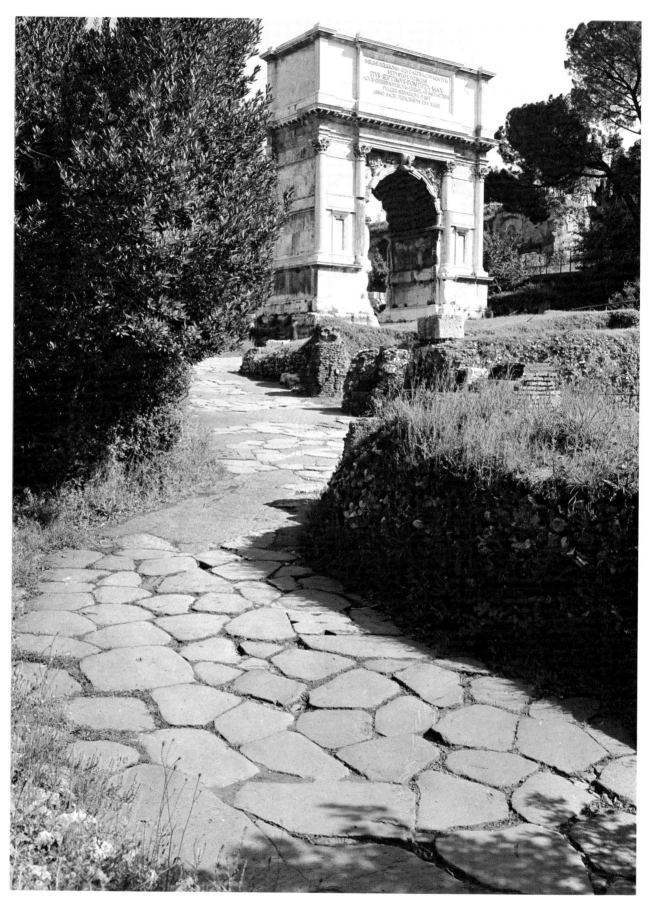

or the temple of the Twelve Gods, restored as we read in the inscription in 368, A.D., the last reaction of paganism. Right under the slope of the Capitol are the three Corinthian columns of the **Temple of Vespasian,** started by Titus and finished by Domitian in 89 A.D., next to it is a platform and a few marble blocks, all that is left of the **Temple of Concord,** dedicated in 367 B.C. to commemorate the victory of the plebians, when the Licinio-Sextian laws were passed, and plebeians were permitted to be elected consuls. That was one of the political victories, which gave the letters S.P.Q.R. their meaning. **S.P.Q.R.** stand for **Senatus Populus Que Romanus,** the Senate and the People of Rome.

Across the modern road which separates the Capitol from the Forum are the eight columns of the **Temple of Saturn,** where the state treasure was kept; the temple was built in 497 B.C.; the Ionic columns of the portico belong to the reconstruction of the IV century A.D. Near the temple of Saturn, under a protective roof, is the Vulcanal, or **Altar of Vulcano,** sacred to the forge, which according to tradition, was founded by Romulus, who made a pact near it with the Sabine

King, Titus Tatius, after the rape of the Sabine women. The other place, which dates from the time of Romulus, which we can still see is the **Comitium,** the small open space between the Curia and the arch of Septimius Severus, where also the **Rostra** was, the platform from which orators used to address the people assembled in the Comitium. In this place we also find the **Lapis Niger,** a black marble stone inserted into the pavement, marking a sacred spot. Beneath the Lapis Niger are kept remains of monuments, among the earliest in the Forum, the so-called **Tomb of Romulus,** and a truncated cone-shaped column with an inscription in archaic Latin letters, which resemble the Greek alphabet.

The superb triumphal **Arch of Septimius Severus** was dedicated in 203 by Caracalla and Geta, his sons, and, after Caracalla killed Geta, he erased his brother's name from the inscription. The present Curia dates from 305 A.D., rebuilt under Diocletian.

The Roman Senate, the Council of the Elders (from Latin «senex» – old), was the most permanent element in the Roman constitution; it may have been started by Romulus who chose 100 of his best sub-

The Arch of Titus and the Sacred Way.

Arch of Titus. The triumph over the Jews and the spoils from the Temple.

jects. At first only patricians were elegible, but later plebeians were also admitted. Under the Republic it was the chief governing body (510 B.C. to 29 B.C.); under the Empire (29 B.C. to 475 A.D.) it lost its independence of action. The senators, who met in the present Curia, were little more than ciphers. Built over the secretariat of the Senate, on the left of the Curia, is the Baroque **church of SS Luca and Martina.** In the open space on the right are the remains of the **Basilica Aemilia,** built in 79 B.C. The basilica is a type of building with a distinctive architecture which played a large part in the life of the Romans; these great public halls, of Greek inspiration, served mainly for general meetings and business transactions, but were also used as lawcourts, like the **Basilica Julia,** on the other side of the Forum, rebuilt by Julius Caesar over the old Sempronia. Near the ruins of the Julian Basilica stands a single column, the last monument added to the Forum and dedicated in 608 A.D. to the Byzantine usurper **Phocas,** who donated the Pantheon to Pope Boniface IV.

Further down, silhouetted against the dark mass of the Palatine, at the far end on the right, soar the three magnificent columns of the **Temple of Castor and Pollux,** the brothers of Helen of Troy, which is one of the oldest temples; it was dedicated in 484 B.C. According to the legend, the twin gods brought to Rome the news of the victory of Lake Regillus, the final victory over the deposed Tarquin dynasty. To the left of the temple of Castor and Pollux, are the ruins of the small circular white **temple of Vesta,** whose cult survived immutable for about a thousand years. In that small temple the sacred fire burnt, symbol of the perpetuity of the Roman State and of the household fire.

These ruins consist of fragments of the last reconstruction of the Vesta temple, in 191 A.D. Behind the temple are the remains of the house of the Vestal Virgins, who kept the fire alive; they were maintained by the State, enjoyed great influence, and after thirty years of austerity, they could leave the order and get married, but if they transgressed the oath of virginity, were entombed alive. On the left of the Vesta Temple are the scanty remains of the **Altar of Caesar,** the altar of the temple built over the spot where the body of Caesar was cremated on the improvised pyre, near the old Rostra, from which Mark Antony delivered his famous oration. At the far end of the Forum on the left, are the high steps and the corinthian columns of the pronaos of the Temple of Antoninus and Faustina, the parents of Marcus Aurelius, the temple was dedicated in 141 A.D. and was made into a Christian Church, dedicated to **San Lorenzo in Miranda;** beyond the columns of the portico in the modest facade of 1602.

Beyond this temple stands another mediaeval Church, Santa Maria Novella, which rose over the ruins of **the temple of Venus and Rome,** buil by Hadrian, and the vast mass of the **Basilica of Constantine or Maxentius** which towers behind it. In the far background stands the **Arch of Titus,** erected in A.D. 81, eleven years after the conquest of Jerusalem, which has a relief representing the spoils of the Temple.

After identifyng the most outstanding landmarks of the Roman Forum let us try and picture something of its early days and comprehend the part which this square played in the history of Rome and in the evolution of mankind. The Forum, as we see, is in a depression of the terrain lying between the Palatine, the Quirinal and the Capitol. The Sabines lived on the Quirinale, Rome was founded by Romulus on the Palatine in 753 B.C. and this valley made from the very beginning a natural meeting point for those primitive people. This supplies the explanation for the center of Rome's development here. The Forum was always revered by the Romans as the cradle of their institutions, as here they established the first elements of an organised society, such as counting, measuring, monetary system, political and religious organisation etc. In the oldest inscriptions the first numbers we find are five and ten, the number of fingers, for measurements they used the length of the foot.

The inhabitants of the pastoral villages on the seven hills counted their wealth in heads of cattle, and that was their first currency. The official rate of exchange, for a long time, was ten sheep to one cow (in Latin sheep is «pecus», from it originated the word pecuniary). The second Roman King, Numa Pompilius, coordinated the State Religion and founded the Vesta Temple; under the kings the buildings in the Forum were mainly of social and religious nature. Under the Republic our Forum became splendid and was the real center of city life, with its basilicas and temples, surrounded by tall buildings and colonnades; lined with attractive shops, and was also the scene of triumphs and sacrifices. With the death of Caesar (44 B.C.) and the accession of Augustus (29 B.C.) the Republic perished and that was the end of the free constitution and the beginning of the decline of the old Forum. With the spoils of the Gallic war Julius Caesar built his new Forum, at the same time as he built the Saepta Julia, great halls for political meetings. Augustus, Nerva, Vespasian and Trajan are the emperors who continued the reconstruction of the center of Rome on a larger scale, (under Trajan Rome had a population of one and a half million inhabitants). The Palatine, which during the Republic had been a fine residential quarter, was occupied by the imperial palaces; it became the new center of the Roman world. After the great days of the Republic, the power of the emperors replaced the power of the Senate, the letters **SPQR** lost their meaning and the voice of the people was never heard again. The old Forum became a place of idle gossip. The tremendous riches extorted from the conquered provinces caused profound psychological changes in the Romans. The

Roman Forum. The ruins of the temples of Saturn and Vespasian and below, a reconstruction of this corner of the Forum, from a design by G. Gatteschi.

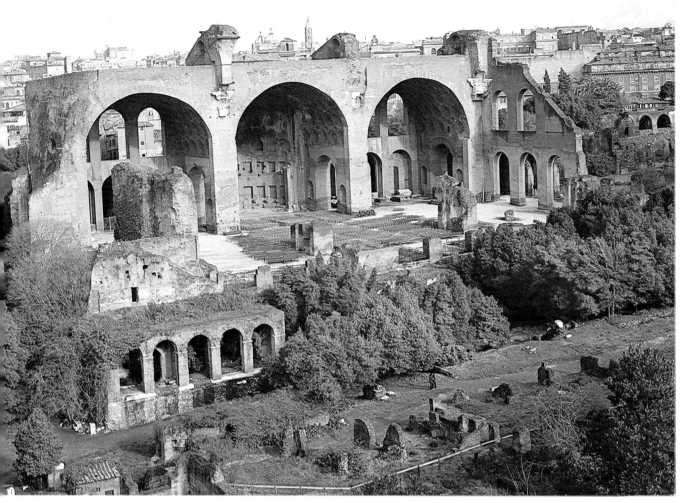

Roman Forum. The remains of the Basilica of Maxentius and below, a reconstruction of the same from a drawing by G. Gatteschi.

The Forum seen from the Palatine. In the foreground the columns of the Temple of Castor and Pollux; further back at the right: the Curia.

most important changes were the decay of their morals and the loss of their stoic virtues of discipline, industry and frugality. The army was formed mainly from barbarian mercenaries, who were led by romanised barbarian commanders. To this add the greed of the soldiers (Claudius raised to the throne by the soldiers in 41 A.D., was the first to give them a salary bonus, which was subsequently exacted as a legal claim on the accession of every new emperor. More than once the Empire was sold to the best bidder by public auction). These are some of the reasons for the decline and fall of the Roman Empire. The mother city of Western Civilisation fell in 475 A.D., was invaded and sacked twice before then, in 410 by the Goths of Alaric and in 455 by the Vandals of Gensceric. It is, in any case, in the ruins of the old Forum, that we see the starting point of the power of Rome, of what we are pleased to call Civilisation, by which we mean the Western World, because Rome is not just the capitol of the ancient world, not just the capital of united Italy, not just the capital of Christianity, but Rome is Ours.

Museum of Roman Civilization. The model of Imperial Rome – reconstruction by the architect I. Gismondi. Detail of the monumental

PIAZZA
VENEZIA

COLONNA
TRAIANA

VIA DEI FORI IMPERIALI

VIA PANIS...

VIA SERPENTI

VIA CAVOUR

V. G. LANZA

VIA DELLE SETTE SALE

MONUM. A VITT. EMANUELE

S. PIETRO
IN VINCOLI

VIALE

MONTE OPPIO

TERME DI TRAIANO

...RCELLO

V. DELLA CONSOLAZIONE

CAMPIDOGLIO

...GARIO

V. DELLA...

V. S. TEODORO

FORO
ROMANO

VIA D. ANNIBALDI

COLOSSEO

VIA LABI...

VIA

VIA

V. CAPO D'AFRICA

SAN

S. GIOVANNI

VIA DE...

TEMPIO
DI VESTA

PALATINO

VIA SAN GREGORIO

V. CLAUDIA

V. ANNIA

V. CELIMONTANA

OSPEDALE
D. CELIO

ROCCA
...TA'

VIA S.

V. S. PAOLO D. CROCE

VIA S. STEFANO

CIRCO MASSIMO

VIA DEI CERCHI

CIRCO MASSIMO

VILLA
CELIMONTANA

V. D. NAVICELLA

...VENTINO

SABINA

CLIVO DEI PUBLICI

PIAZZA
PORTA
CAPENA

FAO

V. TERME DI CARACALLA

PORTA
METRONIA

PORTA
METRO...

VIA SANTA PRISCA

AVENTINO

V. AVENTINA

V.LE G. BACCELLI

VIALE

V. DRUSO

V. M. GELSOMINI

VIALE

V. S. SABA

TERME DI CARACALLA

V.LE G. BACCELLI

VIA ANTONINIANA

VIALE GIOTTO

VIALE PORTA

PORTA
S. PAOLO

ARDEATINA

V. O. BECCARI

VIA MARCO POLO

STAZIONE OSTIENSE

V. MATTEUCCI

VIALE OSTIEN...

EUR

VIA C. COLOMBO

V.LE MURA LATINE

PORTA
S. SEBASTIANO

VIA

BASILICA
S. PAOLO

CATACOMBE DI
DOMITILLA

CATAC...
S. CA...

ROMA

T.P.E. EDITORE - ROMA

area. The Colosseum and the Circus Maximus, and between them, the area of the Fora and the Palatine can be easily distinguished..

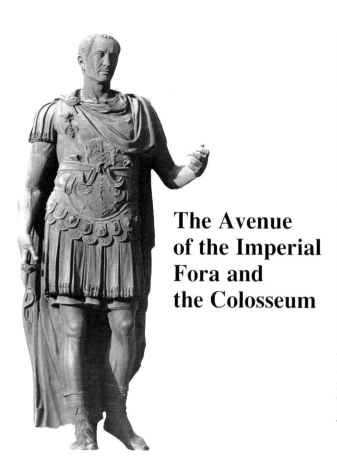

The Avenue of the Imperial Fora and the Colosseum

From the Forum we proceed to the Colosseum and near the Arch of Septimus Severus on the left is **the Mamertine prison,** the old Roman state prison where St. Peter and St. Paul were kept prisoner, and where one of St. Peter's chains was found and where St. Paul wrote his last epistles. Over the prison now stands the small church of St. Joseph and close by are the remains of **Julius Caesar's Forum,** the part of the new city center which he started building. Across the **avenue of the Imperial Fora** are the ruins of the section built by Nerva and by Augustus (there are three columns left of the **Mars Temple**) and the ruins of the enormous market place built by Trajan in 110 A.D. When you have the imposing structure of the Colosseum in front of you, on your right you see the remains of the **Basilica** started by **Maxentius,** and completed by Constantine in the fourth century A.D. On a wall are four marble maps which illustrate the growth of the Roman Empire, from the beginning, in the 8th century B.C. to Emperor Trajan's death in 117 A.D., when the Empire reached its largest extension. Approaching the Colosseum, on the right, you admire the majestic beauty of the **Arch of Constantine,** inaugurated in 315 A.D. It celebrates the final victory of Emperor Constantine and it marks the beginning of Rome as a Christian State.

Via dei Fori Imperiali. The statue of Julius Caesar.

The ruins of the Forum of Julius Caesar, with the three columns of the Temple of Venus.

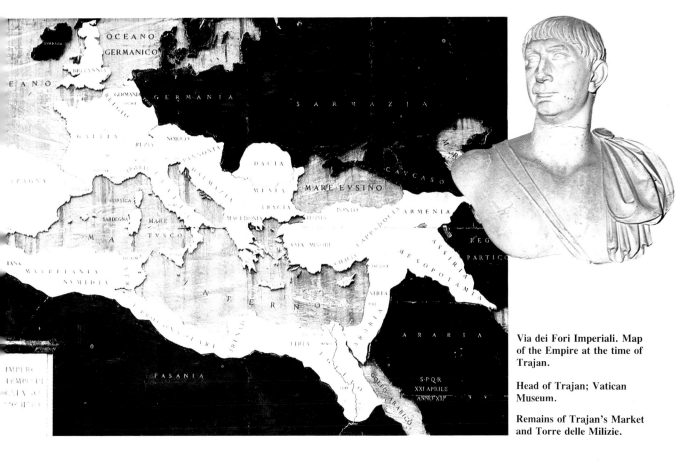

Via dei Fori Imperiali. Map of the Empire at the time of Trajan.

Head of Trajan; Vatican Museum.

Remains of Trajan's Market and Torre delle Milizie.

On the left of the Colosseum is the area, partly occupied by public gardens, laid out over the ruins of **Nero's Domus Aurea.** This part of Rome, before the famous fire, was densely populated and was a large, poor district. On July 18th, 64 A.D. the fire started and Rome burned for six days, leaving thousands homeless. We are not sure that Nero had anything do

Capitoline Museum; Portrait of Nero.

The Naumachia. Nero used to watch naval battles on the lake; later the Colosseum was built on the site, and Romans could watch the same spectacle in the Colosseum itself. Augustus had a Naumachia (lake) constructed near the Gardens of Caesar by the year 2 A.D; later Trajan built another not far from the Vatican.
The 17 century Veronese engraver Onofrio Panvinio has left us this fine reconstruction of a Naumachia.

Arch of Constantine.

The «Colossus», the gigantic statue of Nero, from which the Colosseum takes its name. A drawing by G. Gatteschi.

NAVMACHIAE·IDEST·NAVALIS·PVGNAE

ONVPHRII·PANVINII·VERONEN
AVCTORIS

with it, but, in any case, he profited from the circumstance, and had his fabulous **Golden House** built. The building, alone, covered a square mile in the heart of Rome. Besides the imperial residence there were parks, gardens and baths, supplied by sulphur springs, which were 12 miles away and also supplied by water from the Mediterranean. There was a temple to Fortuna, built of translucent stone and a big, artificial lake for naval battles, to amuse the Emperor. A colossal gilded bronze statue of Nero, one hundred and twenty feet high, stood near the lake. In 68 A.D. Nero was in Greece, showing his abilities as an actor, when the legions in Spain revolted and proclaimed their commander, Galba, emperor. He accepted and marched towards Rome, where the Senate decreed Nero's death. When Nero came back to Rome he found no friends and he ordered his slave to kill him, on June 9th 68 A.D. His house was demolished, the golden colossus was decapitated, and Apollo's head replaced that of Nero and over the site of the artificial lake the Colosseum was built, so named from the gilded colossus.

The Colosseum was begun by Vespasian in 72 A.D. and completed by Titus in 80 A.D. In the year 70 A.D. Titus conquered Jerusalem and brought 100.000 captives to Rome; 40,000 of them built the Colosseum in only eight years. The huge amphitheater could hold about 60,000 spectators, and it was intended mainly for the gladiatorial fights and hunting of wild animals. Captive warriors, when not sold as slaves, or employed by the State in public works, could be given the alternative of performing as gladiators in the arenas of the Empire. After a number of victories, they eventually gained freedom.

For the fights of the gladiators the arena was covered with sand (Latin «arena» - sand). For the hunting of wild animals they used to set up a scene with bushes, trees and hills etc. The wooden floor was supported by the structures, visible when you are inside the Colosseum, and underneath the floor were the dungeons and the beastpens. In the beginning, boat fights were also attempted, but they found it too difficult to flood the arena with water and then dry it up; thus a basin was built elsewhere for them. The Colosseum was used mainly during the warm season and to protect the spectators from the heat a canvas roof (the «Vela-

The Colosseum.

Gladiatorial graffiti discovered at the Colosseum.

VERSO IL TEMPIO DI VENERE E ROMA

VERSO LE TERME DI TITO

VERSO IL LUDUS MAGNUS

0 10 20 30 40 50 60 70 80 90 100 m.

The Colosseum: Interior as it is today.

Recent studies have ascertained that the Colosseum was built on a huge elliptical ring foundation twelve metres thick and fifty metres wide, with a maximum diameter of one hundred and eighty-eight metres, made of concrete and blocks of granite. On this rest the load-bearing pillars of travertine. The enormous underground structure rests in turn on the clay bed of Nero's lake – that is to say on mud which enables it to absorb earth tremors and shifts in the distribution of weight. Even by today's standards it is a magnificent engineering achievement, which explains how the Colosseum has lasted for two thousand years.

The Colosseum: reconstruction of the interior.

rium»), open in the center, was spread over the amphitheater. The Romans watched the cruel performances in the Colosseum until 608 A.D. The Colosseum was made into a fortress during mediaeval times. During the Renaissance it was torn down and much of the stone was used to build palaces and churches. The plundering continued for centuries; and not until the 19th century did the popes start repairing what was still left. We can see very clearly the re-bricked parts.

Apart from the usual arena spectacles, the Colosseum is a perfect example of excellent engineering and fine architecture. Also the Colosseum is based on the principle of the arch, as all Roman architecture is. Il consists of a system of elliptical rings and arches; like the Pantheon it was archieved by a complicated system of relieving arches. To get the whole structure into balance, they had to calculate the strength of each arch in relation to the entire building.

Mosaics of the 3rd century BC with hunting scenes and gladiatorial
combat; Borghese Museum.

The Circus Maximus. Reconstruction. Detail from the model of Imperial Rome in the Museum of Roman Civilization in EUR by I. Gismondi.

A Roman chariot. Vativan Museum.

The Circus Maximus today.

Christians at the Circus. 19th century engraving.

From the Colosseum to St. Paul's without the Walls

Leaving the Colosseum we take Via San Gregorio Magno, between the Palatine and the Caelian hill. On the right are some remains of the acqueduct built by Claudius, and on the left is the **church of St. Gregory the Great.** This site holds the memory of the great Pope, who sent to Britain the band of Benedictines, with Saint Augustine at their head, to evangelize the country. He was also a musician and wrote the Gregorian Chants, and he was the one who had the vision of Archangel Michael over Hadrian's tomb. At the end of Via San Gregorio, you can locate **the Circus Maximus,** in the open space on the right, the valley lying between the Palatine and the Aventine. The remains of the Imperial Palaces, where the aristocracy lived, are on the Palatine (the plebeians lived on the Aventine). The Circus Maximus was the largest stadium for chariot races. It could accommodate over 250,000 spectators. During the persecutions the majority of Christian martyrs were offered there. Now you can only see the site of the arena which was separated into two tracks by a long, low wall, the Spina.

CIRCI.MAXIMI.ET.PALATII.ANTIQVI.IMPERATORVM.ROMANORVM.EX.HIS.QVAE.SVPERSVNT VESTIGIIS RELIC

Monumentis Certiſſima delineatio Onuphry Panuiny Veronenſis

PALATIVM

Templum Matris Deum. Domus Tiberiana   *Moe   nia*

Theatrum Tauri

Hermulus

Carceres

Bigae

Ova Castorum
Obeliscus Iunæ
Delphini
Victoria
Ara Victoriæ
Surculus
Trigus
Vasa Sacra
Genius P. R.
Ara Genii
Ara Murcis
Ara Larium
Neptunus equestris
Mater Deorū

Subsellia

Curious

Spina

Quadrigae

TABERNAE MERCATORVM

CIRCVS   *Meridies versus Auentinum*   M.

Cum Priu. Ordd. Holl.et West - Fris

112

Domus Augustana

Septizonium

Finis Viæ Appiæ

Publica

Col. Sextia

Col. Mathia

Col. Turzelina

Ara Fortunæ

Fortuna

Ora Circulorum

Aedes Solis

Ora Cæsoris

VS

The four charioteers in the famous Roman mosaic in the Terme Museum. The competitors were divided into four groups, and wore different colours. ALBATO (white), RUSSATO (red), PRASINO (light green) and VENETO (pale blue).

San Paolo fuori le Mura
(St. Paul's without the Walls)

We are directed to St. Paul's outside the Walls passing the modern FAO building on our left, (Food and Agricolture Organization of the United Nations) and then we pass St. Paul's gate, which is another gate of the Aurelian Wall. By the gate is the Pyramid of Caius Caestius Epulone, a Roman tomb built in the style of the Egyptian pyramid, in 11 B.C. Almost three hundred years later the pyramid was included in the defensive wall built by Aurelianus. Behind the wall and the pyramid lies the **Protestant cemetery** of Rome where the two English poets, Shelley and Keats, are buried. Then we continue on the old Ostiense Way, the road leading to Ostia, the ancient seaport of Rome. It was the commercial and military harbour of Imperial Rome, at tha time Ostia had a population of one hundred-thousand people. Ancient Ostia is the best preserved Roman city, after Pompei, and modern Ostia is the beach of the Romans.

Emperor Constantine built the Basilica of St. Paul's without the Walls, over the grave of this Saint as a memorial church, as he did over the grave of St. Peter. St. Paul was beheaded at a place called «ad Aquas Salvias», known as le Tre Fontane (the Three Fountains). These three fountains welled up where St. Paul's head had touched the ground and where three churches, tended by the Trappist monks, now stand. After the martyrdom, the Saint was buried near the Ostia road and the church which Constantine built in the IV century was rebuilt more magnificently in 386 and was almost totally destroyed by fire in a few hours on July 15th, 1823, during restoration works of the wooden ceiling. The present basilica was

The pyramid of Cestius at Porta San Paolo.

The Basilica of St Paul's outside the Walls. Main facade.

Interior of the Basilica of St Paul's; lithograph by Benoist, 19th century.

13th century Cosmatesque cloister. St Paul's outside the Walls.

St Paul's outside the Walls. Detail of the mosaic in the apse of Christ Pantocrator. 13th century.

rebuilt as a perfect reproduction of the old one with contributions from different countries. The front of the church is not facing the rising sun, and this is the only one of the patriarchal churches which does not. The present church has a quadriportico which the old one did not have, in the middle of which stands the modern statue of Saint Paul, by Obici. St. Paul is holding a sword in his hand, which is the symbol of the fight he fought for Christianity. You will recall the second letter to Timothy, his last farewell to the Christians: «For I am ready to be offered, my course is finished, I fought a good fight; I have kept the faith... ». The front of the church is decorated with a resplendent mosaic work by the artists of the mosaic studio of the Vatican. The door at the extreme right is the Porta Santa (the Holy Door).

Entering this church you would almost believe it to be the interior of an Imperial Roman basilica, miraculously survived from the past and perfectly preserved through the centuries; it really gives an exact idea of the basilicas of Imperial Rome. Over the main altar

and the Apostle's grave, at which only the Pope celebrates Mass, is the beautiful 13th century altar canopy, by Arnolfo di Cambio, which was rescued from the fire by the triumphal arch over it. This arch had been donated to the church by Galla Placidia, queen of the Goths in the fifth century. The arch, the canopy and the apse, with the 13th century mosaic, are the only remaining parts of the old church. You will also notice the roundels, with the mosaic portraits of all the 264 Popes, including the present one. All the alabaster of the windows was donated by the Viceroy of Egypt. Mohamed Ali, and Czar Nicholas I of Russia contributed the malachite altars at the end walls of the transept.

From the church we pass into the lovely cloister garden in the adjoining monastery. The Benedictine monastery was rebuilt, but the 13th century colonnade in its rich Cosmatesque style is original. All around are the remains of the church which burned and tombstones from the Catacombs and other graves.

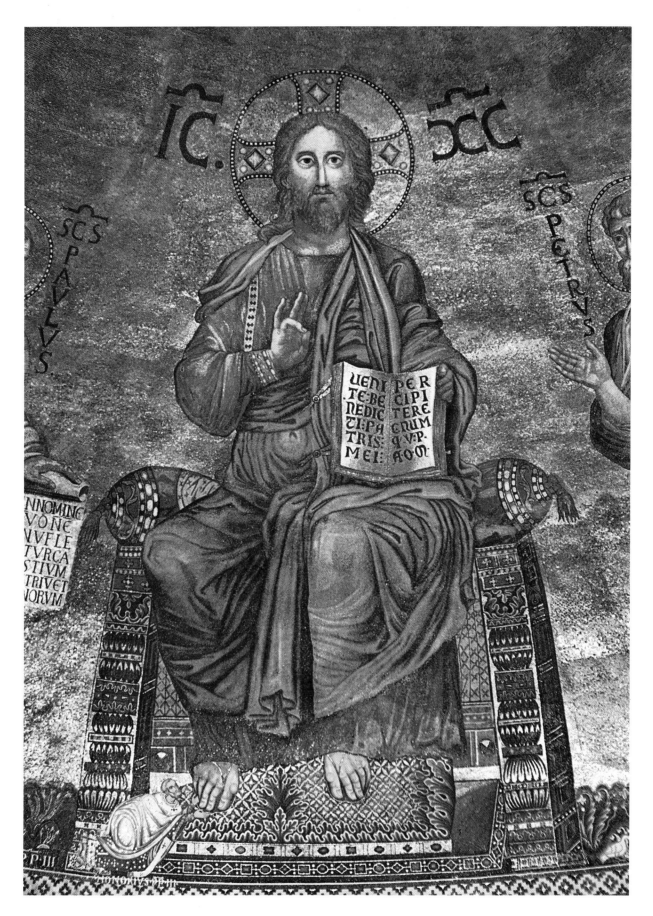

SCS PAVLVS

SCS PETRVS

VENI PER
TE BE CIPI
NEDIC TERE
TI PA CRVM
TRIS QVP
MEI AOM

INNOMINE
VONE
NVFLE
TVRCA
STIVM
TRIVET
NORVM

P III

HONORIVS PP III

fourth tour

Santa Maria Maggiore (St. Mary Major) - Saint Peter in Chains - The Holy Stairs - St. John Lateran - The Appian Way - The Catacombs

Santa Maria Maggiore is one of the four main patriarchal and pilgrimage basilicas with the Porta Santa. It stands on the Esquiline, another of the historical seven hills of Rome, and this is the first church in the West to have been dedicated to the Madonna. It was built first in 352, after the miracle of the snow. In 352 a patrician, named John, and his wife, who both wanted a child, saw the Madonna in a dream. The Madonna told them that their desire was answered and that they should build a church on the site where they would, the next morning, find snow. When they told Pope Liberius of their dream he said that he had dreamed the same dream. In the morning of the 5 th of August the area of the Esquiline Hill was covered with snow (it is very hot in Rome in August).

The present church is the one built under Pope Sixtus III (432-440) to celebrate the Council of Ephesus (431), which proclaimed the Holy Motherhood of the Virgin Mary. In front of it stands a column taken from the Basilica of Maxentius in the Forum which was dedicated to the Madonna in the XVII century. The facade was renovated by F. Fuga in 1743, in late Baroque style, in the portico, on the left, is the Porta Santa.

It is the interior of the church which is really worth seeing; the majestic beauty of its classic architecture was improved by the adornments added later. Of the original building, we still see the 36 columns of Greek marble taken from the temple of Juno, on the Aventine; and above the columns is a series of mosaics from the fifth century, 36 pictures representing events from the Old Testament. They are extremely well preserved, showing a strong classical inspiration and were certainly copied from old miniatures, from old illuminated stories of The Bible. They form, with the ones on the triumphal arch and the decoration of the apse the real glory of Santa Maria Maggiore. The Cosmatesque floor, the finest in that style in our churches,

was added in the thirteenth century and the wooden ceiling, gracefully designed by Antonio da Sangallo, an eminent Renaissance architect, was built at the end of the 15th century. The ceiling was gilded with the first gold Columbus brought from America to Europe. That gold was donated by King Ferdinand of Aragon, of Spain, to the Borgia Pope Alexander VI. Over the papal altar is a huge canopy, probably inspired by Bernini's canopy in St. Peter's, but it certainly is not the finest feature of this church; it was designed by Fuga, the same architect responsible for the 18th century facade. In the lowered part, in front of the papal altar, and in front of the crypt, where are kept the relics of the Holy Cradle, is the kneeling statue of Pope Pius IX, the Pope who declared the dogma of the Immaculate Conception of the Virgin Mary in 1854.

Above the altar are the other fifth century mosaics, which complete the series of the ones in the central nave and depict events from the life of Mary and the childhood of Christ, still referring to the Council of Ephesus: they show less classical influence. The story begins at the top, on the left, with the Annunciation, where the Virgin Mary is unusually represented seated and spinning. The mosaics on the apse are by Torriti, 13th century, strongly influenced by Byzantine art, but the figures lack the absolute flatness of Byzantine style and there is a touch of life in the colourful groups of the angels. The Triumph of Mary and the Coronation are the climax of the other mosaics in this church.

The two large chapels on either side of the High Altar form the transept of the church. The one on the left was built by Pope Paul V Borghese. **The Borghese chapel** is known as the richest private chapel in the churches of Rome. At the main altar is a 13th century icon of the Madonna, held by a glory of angels. The frame is encrusted with precious and semi-precious

119

stones and there is a large display of most valuable marbles all around. Above the altar is the relief with the miracle of the snow. This chapel was decorated in the seventeenth century by the generations which had sponsored the gewgaws of the Baroque style, but without the ostentation of the extreme Baroque. The paintings are by Cavalier d'Arpino and Guido Reni; notice the St. Francis under the arch to the left. In the crypt of the chapel are buried several members of the Borghese family, also Paoline Bonaparte. Opposite is the **chapel of the Holy Sacrament,** built by Domenico Fontana under Pope Sixtus V, in 1585; its gilded-bronze, rich ciborium is by L. Scalzo, and it stands over the remains of the 13th century chapel, where the relics of Jesu's Crib were originally kept. Before leaving the Church we stop for a look at the tomb of Bernini; the founder of the most adorned and elaborate of artistic styles was given a most humble grave, just a simple marble slab with his name on it. He received the honour of resting in this important basilica, which is one of the finest churches in the world, where you find the best examples of the main styles of the last fifteen hundred years. Here, without much effort and with the knowledge of a few essential elements of style, you can enjoy reading the history of the art of fifteen centuries and see how architecture can tell the human story. This classic basilica has first class examples of mediaeval art in the mosaics and the floor, the Renaissance ceiling by Sangallo and the Baroque adornment of the Borghese chapel. All, except the canopy, fit together quite harmoniously.

Interior of Santa Maria Maggiore.

Santa Maria Maggiore. The Baptistery.

Santa Maria Maggiore: Apse with thirteenth century mosaic decoration, and the High Altar with a baldacchino by F. Fuga, eighteenth century.

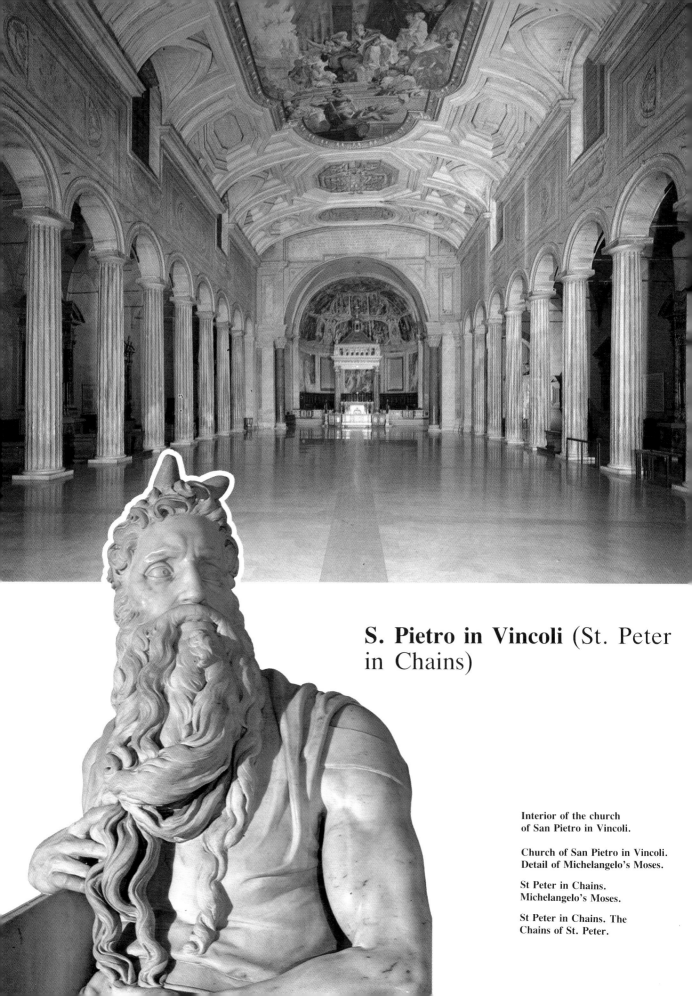

S. Pietro in Vincoli (St. Peter in Chains)

Interior of the church
of San Pietro in Vincoli.

Church of San Pietro in Vincoli.
Detail of Michelangelo's Moses.

St Peter in Chains.
Michelangelo's Moses.

St Peter in Chains. The
Chains of St. Peter.

This church was built about 440 A.D. by Eudoxia, the wife of Emperor Valentinian III to be a shrine for the chains of St. Peter, which she had received from Pope Leo I (The Great). This occured after the chains, one from the Mamertine Prison, near the Forum, and the other from the prison of Jerusalem, where St. Peter was held, according to tradition, were wrought together by miracle. The interior of the church is in the style of a Roman basilica, with 24 beautiful marble columns in Doric style; the ceiling was painted by Parodi, XVII century and the floor has been recently restored. The most important feature of St. Peter in Chains is, in any case, the statue of **Moses by Michelangelo.** He made this statue for Pope Julius II, nephew of Sixtus IV. Sixtus IV, before being elected pope, had been titular cardinal of St. Peter in Chains and this title he gave later to his nephew, Julian della Roverc (ncpotism was the pontifical fashion then). Julian became pope, with the name of Julius II; he is the pope who started rebuilding St. Peter's at the Vatican, who had the ceiling of the Sistine Chapel painted by Michelangelo and had the Stanze painted by Raphael. Well, as soon as Julius II was elected, he started thinking of his magnificent mausoleum to be placed in the new St. Peter's church and he summoned to Rome Michelangelo, who had just astonished his townsmen with the colossal statue of David. Michelangelo planned for the pope a huge monument, which was to be three-storied, four-sided, decorated with 44 statues of the size of Moses and 28 reliefs. The contract was stipulated, Michelangelo was soon off to the Carrara quarries to choose marbles for his gigantic undertaking. He spent seven months there. When Michelangelo came back to Rome, the Pope had changed his mind, ad he had been persuaded by Michelangelo's competitors against the project. He tried, unsuccessfully, to settle with the pope and after a quarrel he left Rome. Later they were reconciled, but he was kept busy with other works, and the monument was never finished. The 44 colossal

statues dwindled to one and Julius II never saw his mausoleum finished.

At length, after innumerable vicissitudes and controversies, in 1545 when Michelangelo was 70, and 40 years after he had made his first plan for the mausoleum of Julius II, he completed the monument we see now in St. Peter in Chains and was finally released from that contract by the relatives of the dead pope. The statue of Moses was probably finished one or two years after he had painted the ceiling of the Sistine Chapel.

The figure of the prophet is very close to the ones he painted on that ceiling; it has the same majesty and power and is one of the many magnified human figures created by Michelangelo, reflecting his concepts of Man and his philosophy. The statue of Moses, more than any other by Michelangelo, embodies his sentiments and thoughts; it portrays exactly the fervent emotions, the anger, the conception, the disappointment and the sorrow of Moses in a dramatic moment of his life, when after receiving the Ten Commandments from God, he came down from Mt. Sinai and found his people worshipping the Golden Calf. Michelangelo has represented in the marble, with perfect exactness, the psychology of that moment. Moses is holding the tables under his right arm tightly, as if to defend from heresy the Code of Law on which the human rights of generations to come would be based.

The Scala Santa and San Giovanni in Laterano
(The Holy Stairs and St. John Lateran)

The Scala Santa: The «Acherotipa» Painting (i.e. «not painted by human hands») of the Saviour, in the Chapel of San Lorenzo. In the Middle Ages it was believed that this picture had been painted by angels.

St John Lateran. Statue of the Emperor Constantine.

The Holy Stairs.

St John Lateran. Main facade and Lateran Palace.

Approaching **St. John Lateran** you notice the Egyptian obelisk which Constantius II brought to Rome in the 4th century, and put in the Circus Maximus as a companion to the one brought by Augustus, nearly four hundred years before and which now stands in Piazza del Popolo. It was re-erected here in 1585 and is the biggest and the oldest one of the fourteen obelisks of Rome. It dates from the fifteenth century B.C. and stood originally before the Temple of Ammon in Thebes. Near the obelisk is the **Lateran Palace,** a Renaissance structure with no other interest than its name and its site. In this palace the Lateran Treaty was signed. It used to house the Lateran Collection, which has recently been moved to the Vatican. It is now the Vicariate. Domenico Fontana, XVI century, is responsible for the architecture. Nearby is the beautiful octagonal Baptistry, built in the V century, and recently restored.

The Laterani, leading noble people of imperial Rome, were the owners of this area, which became property of Constantine as a dowry of his wife, Fausta. After his victory, Constantine gave this area and the palace of Plautius Lateranus to Pope Sylvester in 325 A.D. and so the territorial acquisition of the Church began. The Cathedral of Rome was founded there and for about a thousand years was the seat of the Bishop of Rome. The only remaining parts of the old papal palace are at the top of the Holy Stairs, the **Sancta Sanctorum,** — the Popes' private chapel. The church of the Holy Stairs was originally built in the fourth century to enshrine the staircase, built with the 28 marble steps believed the ones from Pilate's palace in Jerusalem and brought to Rome by St. Helena. Jesus ascended these stairs several times while being judged and descended them to his scouring and death. The faithful climb them on

their knees; Martin Luther, as you know, started up but turned back and walked down. That was his first official sign of protest against the Roman Church. The present church was rebuilt in 1585 by Sixtus V. After getting an impression of the religious significance of the Scala Santa, we walk over to the Cathedral. From far away you have probably watched the giant statues (twenty feet high) at the top of the facade and silhouetted against the Roman sky. They represent Christ, in the Center, and the Doctors of the Church, St. Vincent, St. Ambrose, St. Augustine etc.

The facade of St. John was built by Alexander Galilei in 1735. In the portico is the fourth Porta Santa. The central bronze door, dating from 305 A.D., was moved from the Roman Senate in the Forum, in 1650. At the far inside end of the portico on the left is a restored statue of Emperor Constantine, one of the few statues we have of him. Not even the Romans saw much of Constantine; he was born near the Danube, was educated in Asia and he visited Rome only three times in his life. The church was rebuilt several times and the last reconstruction dates back to 1650, by the Baroque architect **Borromini,** rival of Bernini. The interior appears rather heavy and has imposing statues of the Apostles in the recesses against the piers of the central nave. The statues are by followers of Bernini and above the piers are the reliefs by Algardi, depicting analogies of the Old and New Testament. From the previous reconstructions is the Cosmatesque floor dating from XIV century. The ceiling is by **Daniel da Volterra,** a disciple of Michelangelo, XVI century. The canopy of the High Altar has a touch of Gothic and dates from the XV century. In the canopy beyond the gilded grill, are kept the skull bones of St. Peter and

St John Lateran: the apse and Pope's Throne.

This inscription on the facade of the Basilica, reaffirms its position: «... Mother and head of all the churches of Rome and of the World».

Basilica of St John Lateran and monument to St Francis of Assisi.

St John Lateran: interior.

St. Paul, in the head of the statues of the saints. In the lowered part in front of the main altar is the bronze grave of Pope Martin V (Colonna). (The founder of this princely house was a crusader who brought to Rome from Jerusalem the column of the Scourging of Christ).

In the transept on the left is the altar of the **Blessed Sacrament,** above this are the relics of the table of Jesus's Last Supper. On the right is the monumental pipe organ, from 1598. At the end of the last century the apse was rebuilt; and there is the Throne of the Bishop of Rome.

Above the Papal Throne (**The Cathedra**) is a reproduction, of the 13th century mosaic by Torriti, and the two new pipe organs. This church certainly cannot compete with the classic beauty and authentic antiquity of Santa Maria Maggiore, but from the historical point of view, this is the most important of all the Christian churches.

Its rank is "«Head and Mother» of all Churches in Rome and in the World". It was built, as we saw, as a cathedral and not as a memorial church. This is the seat of the Pope. When the Pope goes out of the Vatican, for the first time after his Coronation, he goes St. John's to take possession of it. This church certainly saw its greatest splendour during the Middle Ages, when the Lateran was still the residence of the Popes. Then the Papacy was driven out of Rome by the riots and violence, and when the Pope came back to Rome after the captivity in Avignon, the Papal Palace of the Lateran had been completely ruined by fire and was uninhabitable and the Pope went to live at the Vatican.

Before leaving the church notice the painting by **Giotto.** Behind the first pier, on the right of the central nave, we have the restored fresco painting of **Pope Boniface VIII** announcing the beginning of the first Holy Year in the history of the Church in 1300, painted by Giotto, who came to Rome for the Jubilee Year.

The Emperor Caracalla. Capitoline Museum.

The Baths of Caracalla.

The Baths of Caracalla and the ancient Appian Way

The Church of «Quo Vadis» on the Via Appia Antica.

To reach the ancient Appian Way and the Catacombs we will pass the imposing remains of the **Baths of Caracalla.** These were the second largest public baths of Imperial Rome, next to those built one hundred years later by Diocletian. They were built by Emperor Caracalla in 206 A.D. In Rome there were eleven of these enormous structures.

The Thermae (baths) were a kind of huge club houses, used mainly for bathing, where the Romans used to entertain. These baths were the most richly decorated; a lot of works of art were recovered from their remains, sculptures and mosaics, which can be seen in the museums of Rome and Naples. In the summer we have there the open-air opera at night. If you happen to be in Rome in July or August you should not miss seeing Aida there. Driving by, you can send a reverent salute to the English poet, Shelley, who in the spring of 1819 wrote most of his «Prometeus Unbound», «upon the mountainous ruins of the Baths of Caracalla».

As soon as you pass these ruins you enter the **ancient Appian Way,** the first military road built by the Romans. It was built to connect Rome with the southern part of Italy, especially with Capua, north of Naples, which was the second most important Italian city in the 4th century B.C. It was then completed as far as Brindisi (Brundisium) on the Adriatic coast and also became the shortest route to the Near East. Brindisi was the sea-port from which the Romans sailed to Greece, Turkey, etc. The road was started in 312 B.C. by Consul Appius Claudius. These were the first miles of the huge network of highways the Romans left over the Empire, in total some

60 thousand miles of road. (After the fall of Rome no new roads were built in Europe for about 15 centuries), 85 Roman bridges are still in use. During the days of the Empire, the first ten miles of the Appian Way were lined with the monumental graves of patrician Roman families. These ten miles formed quite a monumental approach to the capital of the Empire. The Romans were not allowed to bury their dead in the city; they built their tombs along the roads and most of them were on the Via Appia. After we have passed the **tomb of the Scipio family** (the family of warriors, Scipio the Aemilianus, Scipio the Africanus, etc.) we see the **arch of Drusus,** another warrior, better known as Germanicus because of his victories on the Rhine. He was the younger brother of Tiberius, married to Mark Antony's daughter Antonia, and was the father of Claudius, whom Agrippina poisoned to get the throne for her son Nero. Next comes the turreted **gate of S. Sebastian,** the largest and best preserved of the gates in the Aurelian Wall.

Down further on the left is the small famous Chapel of **Domine Quo Vadis,** built over the site where, according to tradition, St. Peter, fleeing from death during Nero's persecution, had the vision of Christ and uttered the famous three words «Domine Quo Vadis» (Lord, where goest Thou) and The Lord replied he was on his way to Rome to be crucified again because Peter had abandoned the Christians in a moment of danger. Peter went back to Rome and was crucified. The chapel was rebuilt in the XVII century by the Barberini family. Two more minutes drive and you are at the Catacombs.

129

Catacombs of St Callius. Statue of St. Cecilia.

Church of St Sebastian. The stone with the imprints of Christ's feet, discovered, according to Christian tradition, in the place where St Peter saw the vision of Christ, and where the «Quo Vadis» chapel was later built.

Catacombs of St Sebastian. One of the galleries.

Catacombs of St Sebastian. Statue of St Sebastian.

The Catacombs

There are about fortyfive Catacombs around Rome, and the most frequently visited are those along the Appain Way; St. Calixtus, St. Sebastian and the Domitilla Catacombs. They are tended by different religious orders and the areas are under the jurisdiction of the Vatican State. There are Pagan, Jewish and, of course, the Christian Catacombs. The term Catacomb was originally applied only to those of St. Sebastian. The others were merely called cemeteries (from Greek koimeterion – a sleeping chamber or burial place).

The majorty of the Catacombs are Christian because Christians liked to be buried in the same way as Christ: in a cave, wrapped in linen, and also because most of the classes and could not afford rich mausoleums. The underground galleries were dug because the surface area could not be exceeded, so they dug more deeply underneath. This explains the five or six levels of the Catacombs. The total estimated length of the galleries is about 500 miles, and about six million people were buried in a span of three hundred years and were known to everyone, but the Roman law was very clear and compassionate about graves. Burial places were considered sacred and nobody could touch or violate them, that is the reason why persecuted Christians would occasionally escape to those underground labyrinths.

Some tours will go to the Catacombs of St. Callixtus, others to those of Domitilla or St. Sebastian.

The Catacomb of St. Calixtus is one of the largest, and in the third century it became the official cementery of the Christian Church; several Popes were buried there. The inscriptions on their graves are very simple, and most of theam are written in Greek, which was the first official language of the Church. Saint Cecilia is buried in this Catacomb. She is the patron saint of musicians. According to tradition, she heard such heavenly sounds that to express them she invented the organ. The Saint was martyred with the heat of the steam bath in her patrician house in Trastevere, where the Church of St. Cecilia now stands. After many hours, without being harmed. she was finally beheaded, but her head could not be severed. In 1599 her coffin was opened and her body was found intact. The sculptor Stefano Maderno made the statue of the Saint exactly as he saw her. This is the replica you see in the crypt—the original is in the Church at Trastevere.

Catacomb of St. Sebastian. In this Catacomb on the Appian Way, during the persecution of Emperor Valerianus, the relics of St. Peter and St. Paul were moved for safe-keeping, so that the place became an object of cult and pilgrimage, confirmed by the «graffiti» written on the walls by the pilgrims; «Peter and Paul pray for us», «Peter and Paul remember us», etc. St. Sebastian is one of the saints of whom you are more frequently reminded, all through Europe, as all art collections have one or more pictures of the martyr, his beautiful young body stuck with arrows. He was a Gaul of Narbonne, an officer in Diocletian's army. The church of St. Sebastian was built over his grave, and there is also the original marble from the site of the Domine Quo Vadis, with the foot-print of Christ.

Domitilla Catacomb. In this very large Catacomb, are fine paintings. You enter it from the basilica, built at the end of the IV century in honour of the Saints Nereus and Achilleus. The area of this Catacomb is called that of Ampliatus. In 1881 a tomb was discovered with the name «Ampliati» engraved in Roman lettering; he is possibly the same Ampliatus mentioned by St. Paul in his «Epistle to the Romans» — «Salute Ampliatus my beloved in The Lord»... In each one of the Catacombs, the fathers provide excellent guides. You will certainly feel the atmosphere of utter faith and complete trust of the early Christians as witnessed by the innumerable inscriptions and paintings, all expressing Christian brotherhood and charity. Continuing further along the ancient Appian

The Good Shepherd, in the Catacombs of St. Domitilla. Fresco painting of the III cent. A.D.

Via Appia Antica. Tomb of Cecilia Metella.

Catacombs of St Domitilla. Underground basilica of St. Nereus and St. Achilleus of the 4th century AD.

Via Appia Antica. Even today, this historic road offers views like this, which inspired the painters of the Romantic school.

Way you pass the remains of the **Circus of Maxentius**, the Emperor defeated by Constantine. He built a stadium for chariot races in the fourth century, A.D., near the mausoleum he built for his son, Romulus, who died at the age of nine. Then the most imposing of the graves which lined the historical road, the **tomb of Cecilia Metella**, daughter of the Roman General Quintus Metellus, called Creticus for he had conquered the island of Crete. Cecilia was married to one of the sons of Crassus, the wealthy Roman who paid Julius Caesar's debts and shared the triumph with him. The grave, built in the first century B.C. and so familiar a landmark of the Roman Campagna, was given by Pope Boniface VIII Caetani to his relatives, who made it into a donjon. They also had the bright idea of building a bridge across the road to exact a toll from travellers to and from Rome. A bit further along the road, parts of original paving, with large cobble-stones are visible.

The historical picturesque promenade will remind you of the many descriptions of the Appian Way by Horace Walpole, Nathaniel Hawthorne, Robert Browning and Lord Byron. Music lovers will recall the Pines of Rome by Respighi, the last part of the melody being inspired by the trees of the Appian Way.

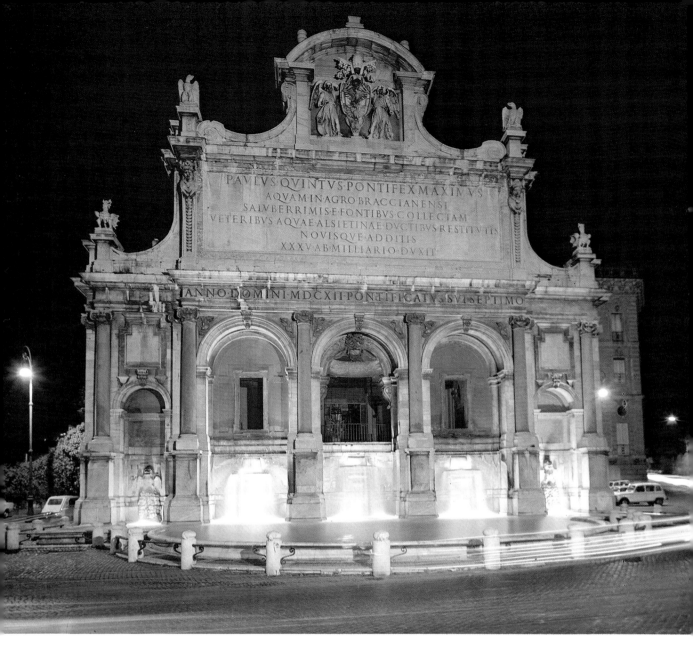

No visit to Rome would be complete without taking in the panoramic view of the city from high up on the Janiculum Hill, the hill which the Romans dedicated to Janus, the God with two faces. In the large open space on the highest point of the hill there stands the equestrian statue of Giuseppe Garibaldi by Gallori, and this stands at the centre of the busts of his soldiers, the «Garibaldini», which are scattered all around the park, as a memorial to the defence of the Roman Republic during the Risorgimento, Italy's nineteenth century national resurgence.

From this piazza we can see the domes and roofs of Trastevere, the old quarter which spreads out at the foot of the hill. Trastevere (from Trans-Tiberin, the other side of the Tiber) was the centre of Rome's oriental community in classical times — and especially of the Jews. It has been inhabited without a break for more than two thousand years, and is considered to be the most «Roman» of all the districts of Rome.

Its inhabitants, known as the «Trasteverini» boast that they are the only authentic descendants of the true Roman stock. In the huddle of old houses, in the mediaeval churches and monasteries and in the buildings of the Renaissance, we can see the evidence of Trastevere's thousands of years of history, but the spirit of the Trasteverini themselves is felt most of all in the typical local haunts where one can still hear the characteristic slang used by Belli and Trilussa, and the natives of the area still keep up the traditional ways and folklore of the area, despite the sophistication which has crept in recent years because of the many colonies of foreigners who now live there.

Among the churches of Trastevere we should mention Santa Maria in Trastevere in particular. It stands on one side of the square named after it, and it is outstanding for its mediaeval structure and for the mosaics and the wealth of other treasures which it possesses.

The Acqua Paola fountain on the Janiculum. 17th century, built on the orders of Pope Paul V (Borghese).

Janiculum
and Trastevere

Santa Maria in Trastevere: The splendid ceiling in inlaid and gilded lacunary style, with the painting of the Assumption by Domenichino.

The Church of Santa Maria in Trastevere.

135

Highways which takes its name from Tibur (ancient Tivoli). This road continues across the Appennines over to Pescara on the Adriatic coast; the first miles of the road are lined with economic housing or small factories and until our first stop we see very little of historical or artistic interest. After we pass the sulphur-water springs, the Acque Albule, and the quarries of travertine stone, the same quarries which supplied the travertine blocks to build the Colosseum, we'll turn right and cross the old, restored Roman bridge, **Ponte Lucano**. Near this bridge over the Aniene, the tributary of the Tiber which feeds the fountains of Villa d'Este, stands the imposing Tomb of the Plautii from the I century, B.C. Then we enter **Villa Adriana**.

fifth tour
Tivoli – Hadrian's Villa and Villa d'Este

After the four tours dedicated to the exploration of churches, museums and ruins, it will be relaxing to drive out to the Roman Campagna, away from the strident roar of the city.

Leaving for Tivoli we'll pass the modern railway station, **Stazione Termini**, noting the remains of the old city wall, known as **the Servian Wall**, the oldest defence wall of Rome, built in the IV century B.C.; **the University City**, completed in 1953 (about 100.000 students), and the mediaeval church of **S. Lorenzo Fuori le Mura**, another Basilica ad Corpus (Basilica at the Body) founded by Constantine over the grave of St. Lawrence. It was renovated in the XIII century and was bombed in 1943, and afterwards restored. We are now on the **Tiburtina** Way, one of the Roman

Hadrian's Villa

This imperial residence was started in the year 125 A.D. and was finished in 135 A.D., though other buildings were added later. Emperor Hadrian, one of the greatest personalities of the Roman world, a great soldier, a statesman, an architect and a poet, was also a great traveller, one of the few Emperors who visited every province of his immense Empire, he inherited from his adoptive father, Trajan, in 117 A.D. However Greece was his great love, which also dominated his architectural ideas, as you may recall from your visit to the Pantheon and as it is evident in the remaining parts of the villa we are going to visit.

The model of the Villa Adriana, recently made, and which we'll see first, will help us to visualise its original appearance. There we see the reproduction of the 25 buildings which formed the residence and in which, according to tradition, the Emperor wished to reproduce outstanding monuments from the various parts of the Empire. Although there is no evidence of these buildings being replicas of others, some resemblance can be found in some of them. The huge wall, standing nearby, sustained the roof of the long-covered walk of the perystile with a central pool, named **Poecile,** from the famous portico of Athens which was decorated with paintings by the most prominent Greek artists. As soon as we find ourselves beyond the long honeycombed tufa wall, we realise the enchantment of Villa Adriana, we are in a real «classical landscape with ruins», one of the places which inspired the English-landscaped parks, and which also gave inspiration to the painters of half Europe. This is perhaps the reason why Hadrian's Villa holds an immediate, magic appeal for the visitor. Throughout the ruins the predominant characteristic will be its interpenetration of vegetation and ruins similar to the original very close asso-

ciation of house and garden, as we saw in the model. For a serious study of Roman architecture there are places, such as Pompei and Ancient Ostia, where buildings are in a much better state of preservation, but much pleasure, I believe, can be gained simply by wandering through the ruins of Villa Adriana, without any knowledge of them. The pathetic remains of these buildings, the broken columns, the fragments of antique reliefs and mosaics, or marble floors, lying half concealed by the colored carpet of field flowers, will console the layman for the difficulty of identifying the component parts of Hadrian's varying architectural lines. We'll continue as far as **the Canopo** inspired by a place of that name near Alexandria in Egypt (a valley with a canal lined with porticoes and shops), and decorated with Greek cariatides.

The only part of Hadrian's Villa to retain any evidence of its past splendour is the **Teatro Marittimo** (the Maritime Theater), built in the form of a circular portico, enriched by the Ionic columns and showing most perfect proportions. It lies between the

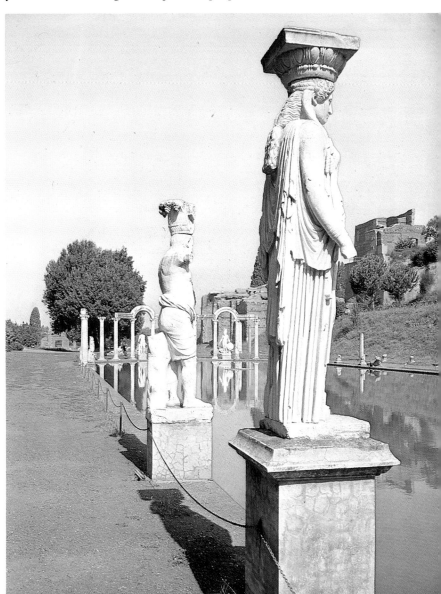

Portrait of the Emperor Hadrian.

Model of Hadrian's Villa by I. Gismondi.

Hadrian's Villa: the Canopus.

All museum of note in the world have something from Hadrian's Villa. The Emperor did not live long enough to enjoy the place created by his genius and originality, in the last months of his life, he went to die at Baiae, (138 A.D.) on the sunny Bay of Naples, where he composed his address to his Soul, the famous five lines later to be written on his grave:

Animula, vagula, blandula,
Hospes comesque corporis,
Quae nunc abibis in loca,
Pallidula, rigida, nudula,
Nec ut soles dabis jocos?

By Charles Merivale we have a very accurate translation:

Libraries and the Hall of the Greek Philosophers. Emperor Hadrian had filled this place with innumerable works of art, and already in the late period of the Empire, the plundering started and continued for centuries; a real gold-mine for archaeologists.

Soul of mine, pretty one, flitting one,
Guest and partner of my clay,
Whither wilt thou hie away,
Pallid one, rigid one, naked one
Never to play again, never to play?

Hadrian's Villa: a capital.

Hadrian's Villa: the maritime theatre.

Villa d'Este

After Villa Adriana we reach Tivoli, through the rather steeply rising road flanked by the very old olive trees. Tivoli, the ancient Tibur, was already occupied by the Romans in the IV century B.C. It is located on the Tiburtine hills, the foothills of the Appennines, the range of mountains crossing all Italy from the French border to the tip of the boot. Tivoli was always a resort place for the Romans; in ancient times prominent personalities and emperors, such as Sallustius, Oratius, Maecenas, Trajan and Hadrian, built their villas there.

From the square where we park we see a XV century fortress, the Rocca Pia, built by Pope Pius II. Tivoli has numerous antiquities and mediaeval structures, but its main attraction is the **Villa d'Este** with its fountains.

This villa was the creation of Cardinal Ippolito d'Este of Ferrara, son of Alfonso d'Este and Lucrezia Borgia; a shrewd diplomat who played an important role in the political and ecclesiastical events of his time, and gained the Cardinal's hat; in 1550 he received the governorship of Tivoli. The place didn't have much to offer to a man brought up in the splendour of a princely court, and with an inborne taste for art and refinement, so he started immediately to build his magnificent palace, out of an old Benedictine cloister adjoining the medieval church of S. Maria Maggiore. There he would be surrounded by artists and men of culture, and following the fashion of the great Roman families of the XVI century, he had his pleasure gardens laid out on the slope of the hill, for which an entire section of the town was demolished. On the spacious terraces of his villa the Cardinal and his humanist friends would stroll, discussing the works of the classical poets.

The plan of the villa was designed by Pirro Ligorio and was carried out by G. Galvani; the fresco painting decoration was executed by G. Muziano, F. Zuccari and L. Agresti, and the sculptures, with which the gardens were adorned, were supplied by

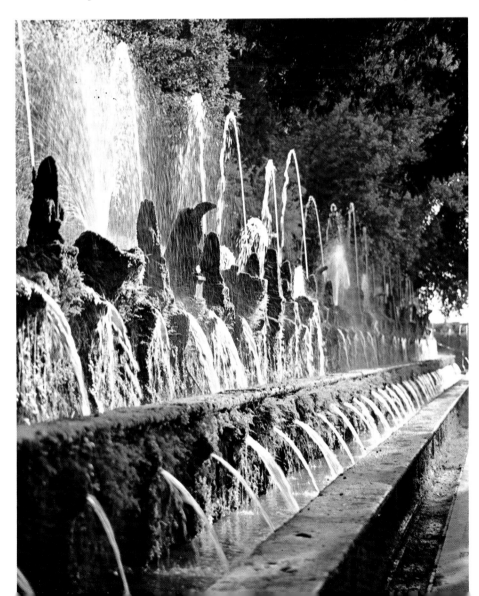

The Villa d'Este: the road of one hundred fountains.

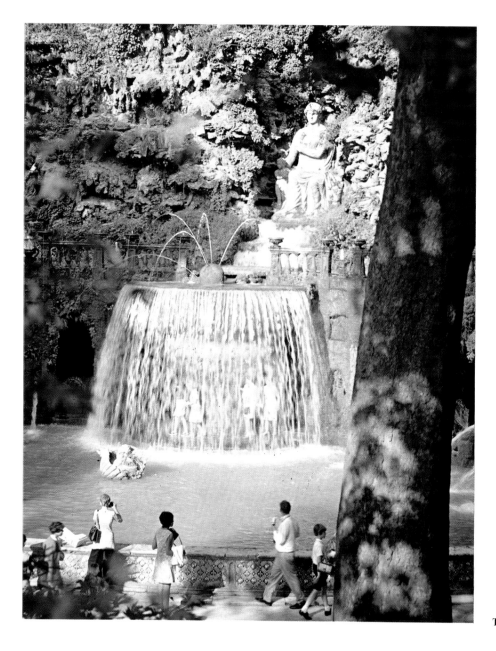

the excavations from the neighbouring Villa Adriana.

Sculptors and engineers contributed to the instalment of fountains, water-falls and pools, and to feed them, two canals were dug to collect the water of the Aniene and of the Rivella. The fountains still work on the original hydraulic system.

The Villa remained the property of the d'Este family until Ercole III d'Este left it to his only daughter Maria Beatrice, wife of the Archduke Ferdinand of Austria and thus the Villa passed to the Hapsburgs, and then in turn to the Hohenlohe family. In the last century extensive hospitality was given in the Villa to famous Austrian artists, Franz Liszt among them. At the beginning of World war I the Italian State confiscated it, finding it neglected and deprived of its

most valuable ornaments. Restorations gave the villa its original aspect and the waterworks were repaired. In the recent years the water-jets have been floodlit (four days a week from April to October).

Passing through the XV century courtyard of the Benedectine monastery, we'll go down to the lower apartment, crossing the central hall, with frescoes by Muziano and Zuccari and a pretty fountain, with simulated rocks and mosaic works. Just outside this room an extensive view of the old part of Tivoli, opens up and away in the distance are the towns of Sant'Angelo Romano and Palombara.

Walking down the paths lined with trees, we'll discover the magnificent fountains which have made this place unique in the world. The most spectacular of them are: the **Fountain of Rometta** (Fountain of little

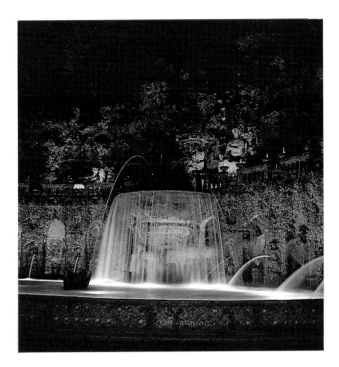

The Villa d'Este: The Ovata fountain at night.

Rome), decorated with midget reproductions of famous ancient Roman buildings: the walk of **One Hundred Fountains,** with the long wall of the avenue turned into a fantasy of ships, obelisks, eagles and fleur-de-lis (these latter are a part of Este's coat-of-arms); from them water-jets fall into the lower level; the **Fountain of the Hydraulic Organ,** is the culmination of the gardens of Villa d'Este, a marvel of hydraulic engineering. This fountain could play music when the water passed through the pipes of a huge organ. When we are at the bottom level we get a better idea of the size of the cypress trees, the tallest in Italy.

On the central axis of the gardens, at mid-level, is the **Fountain of the Dragons;** the statues of the dragons, were, according to tradition, put there overnight, when Pope Gregory announced to the Cardinal his intention of visiting the villa in 1572. The dragon was on the Pope's coat-of-arms.

The Fountain of the Ovata has a most theatrical effect; in it the work of man merges with nature with the greatest harmony.

The Villa d'Este: Rometta fountain; the goddess Roma enthroned. Detail.

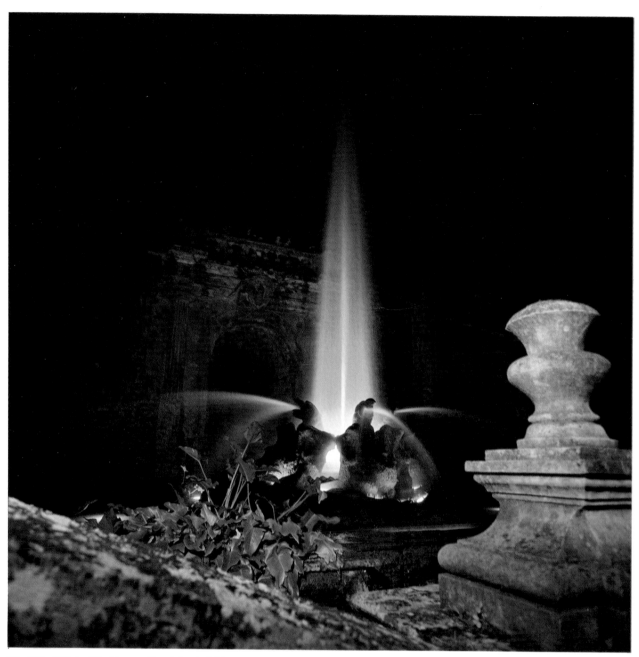

The Villa D'Este: The Dragon Fountain at night.

The Villa d'Este: Fountain of the Pipe Organ.

*Testi di Tullio Polidori - Grafica di Beppe Fontana
Fotografie di: Bruno Fiorina, Sin Ici Wakazuki,
Osvaldo Ottaviani, Bruno del Priore e archivio
dell'editore.
Stampa: Officine Grafiche Calderini - Bologna -
Milano - Roma*